YESTERDAY
THEY TOOK
MY BABY

YESTERDAY THEY TOOK MY BABY

True stories of adoption

BEN WICKS

Stoddart

First published in 1993 by
Stoddart Publishing Co. Limited
34 Lesmill Road
Toronto, Canada
M3B 2T6
(416) 445-3333

Canadian Cataloguing in Publication Data

Wicks, Ben, 1926-
Yesterday they took my baby

Includes index.
ISBN 0-7737-2746-9

1. Adoption — Canada — Psychological aspects.   I. Title.

HV875.58.C2W54 1993   362.7'34   C93-094053-9

Cover design: Brant Cowie/ArtPlus
Typesetting: Tony Gordon Ltd.
Printed and bound in the United States of America

*Stoddart Publishing gratefully acknowledges the support of the
Canada Council, The Ontario Ministry of Culture, Tourism, and
Recreation, Ontario Arts Council and Ontario Publishing Centre in
the development of writing and publishing in Canada.*

Contents

Acknowledgements

Without the help of a huge number of people, this book would have been impossible to write. Where to start is easy — with the hundreds of adoptees, birth parents, adoptive parents and professionals who opened their lives to me, a complete stranger. In doing so they have helped reveal the joy and anguish inherent in the adoption triad. My only regret is that, due to the tremendous response to my appeal for stories, it is impossible for me to thank them all individually or to use all their accounts in this book.

Many newspapers and magazines made it possible for me to appeal to members of the adoption triad to share their stories: the *Toronto Star, Woman's Realm,* various adoption-related newsletters and others too numerous to mention. Several adoption organizations and their many volunteers were always more than willing to do what they could to help, including the many new friends I made in Philadelphia at the American Adoption Congress conference.

My sincere thanks to those involved in adoption issues who went out of their way to assist me: Joyce Cohen, Elaine Rutherford, Valerie Hamilton, Peter Baddeley, Alan Burnell, Anne Marie Karch, Holly Kramer, Jone Carlson, Patricia Sanders, Raymond Ensminger and many more. Particular appreciation is extended to Judith Kizell-Brans, the director of Parent Finders in Ottawa, who was always there to answer my many questions. And David Wong's computer skills were a great help in keeping my records straight.

Once again special thanks go to Sandra Tooze, for her remarkable assistance in researching, shaping and editing the manuscript. As always Matie Molinaro, my Canadian agent for twenty years, and Carolyn Brunton, my London agent, steered me through business jungles that continue to mystify me.

And I thank my wife Doreen who, despite her own incredible agenda to help those in desperate need in the developing world, was always ready to give encouragement.

Introduction

I am not adopted. My life began in the arms of a Cockney mother in the East End of London, and I am fortunate that I stayed within reach of those arms until my mother died at 94 years of age.

Yet my life bears a resemblance to those of many children who were adopted. In 1939, along with thousands of other British children, I was evacuated to the safety of the English country-side, away from German bombing targets. For almost three years I lived in a succession of four different homes. Although I had the comfort of knowing I had a family to go back to, I experienced something of the feelings of alienation suffered by many adoptees. My mother lived with the anguish of surrendering her only son, albeit temporarily, to provide him with a more secure life.

After writing five books of oral history on the Second World War and wishing to write next about a different subject, I conceived the idea for this book when a close friend reminded me that he was adopted. Over lunch he explained that since his adoptive parents, whom he loved dearly, were now dead he felt comfortable in setting out to find his birth parents. Throughout the next two months I received a week-by-week update on his progress. It was an extraordinary story, a rollercoaster ride between the heights of euphoria and the depths of dejection, which finally ended in success. Surely, I thought, if his story was that remarkable there must be others with similar stories to tell.

Not only did I find this to be true, but I was astonished by the enormous numbers of people affected by adoption. Since the first modern adoption law in the English-speaking world was enacted in Massachusetts in 1851, one in eight people has been touched by adoption in the United States. It has been estimated that in the U.S. there are approximately six million adoptees, twelve million birth parents and twelve million adoptive parents, which in total make up twelve and a half percent of the population.

Canada's first children's welfare legislation was passed in 1893 with the Child Protection Act of Ontario. The act, however, did not apply to adoption but to the child boarders and apprentices who had immigrated from Britain. The Ontario Adoption Act was enacted in 1921 to protect orphaned and illegitimate youngsters following World War I. It made no mention of sealed records, but a second act, passed in 1927, introduced severe restrictions on disclosure information; for the first time all records were sealed.

Soon all provinces had similar adoption legislation. Since that time there have been over 200,000 adoptions in Ontario alone.

To this day adoption legislation varies from province to province, and there is no federal policy. The first federal study of adoption in Canada, the National Adoption Study, conducted by Kerry Daly and Michael Sobol of the University of Guelph (*Globe and Mail*, December 1, 1992), will be released in the spring of 1993. Statistics have revealed that while thirty years ago sixty percent of children born to unmarried women under twenty-five were placed for adoption, by 1981 the numbers had dropped to ten percent and nine years later to less than four percent.

The current trend is for more unwed mothers to keep their children. Among those who do not do so, a growing number are choosing to place their infants through private adoption agencies who offer "open" policies. Under open adoption, the birth mother can select the adoptive parents for her baby, meet them and even stay in touch with her child through the exchange of letters, photographs and visits. Some mothers feel this gives them more control over the welfare of their children. Others prefer to use public agencies, feeling that the government organizations do more research into the backgrounds of the adopting parents.

But this is not a book written by an academic schooled in the subject of adoption. By travelling throughout Canada, Britain and the U.S., I had the opportunity to meet and interview those who are perhaps the greatest experts in this particular field: the birth parents, the adoptive parents and — the central figures in any adoption — the adoptees who have experienced firsthand the pain and the happiness of being part of the adoption triangle. It is their stories (frequently under assumed names to protect the feelings of loved ones) that I present to you.

Although often a source of joy and love, adoption has, in the past, equally often fostered intense anger, guilt, grief and alienation. Until fairly recently, young, unmarried mothers were generally forced to relinquish their babies. The social stigma involved, and the absence of material and moral support, offered them virtually no choice. Lives, once joined by the most instinctive bond between parent and child, were split apart. There was never any misunderstanding on the birth parents' side. They knew that, once relinquished, the child became another's responsibility, leaving them with a nagging sense of loss in spite of society's reassurance that what was being done was in the best interests of the child. Any remorse or sense of guilt that might have caused the mother to change her mind was discounted by a system that considered adoption to be the only responsible decision. Adoption records were sealed, making the chances of a planned reunion seem impossible.

For the birth mother, the despair of having relinquished her child continues to haunt her. Living without knowing the welfare of the baby she surrendered still torments her as each birthday marks another milestone in the life from which she is severed. Did she make the right decision?

Largely ignored in many discussions concerning adoption are the adoptive parents. They give so much of their lives to the welfare of their adopted child, fearing, yet fully aware, that the day may come when their son or daughter will feel the need to find his or her birth family. Will there be enough love to go around?

Completing the triangle are millions of adoptees, some who suffer a perpetual anguish from not knowing who they really are. For those of us who were raised by our birth parents, it is difficult to understand the emotions experienced by most adoptees. Many adoptees feel a gap inside, a missing piece of their identity, that must be filled. Others have no desire to find their birth parents and are happy to lead a life that, for them, began when their adoptive parents became the only family they needed.

Although some adoptees succeed in searching out their birth families, many others are still trying to trace the facts of their birth, which continue to give them pain. Today, as adults, they grapple with the issues inherent in the questions: What are my roots? Why was I given up? What are my genetic strengths and weaknesses? Do my birth parents ever think of me?

To find the answers we must go back to the beginning.

1

Mom, I'm Pregnant!

*When I found out I was pregnant I
thought this just couldn't be true. My
becoming pregnant was the worst thing
I could have done, next to murder.*

Rishy Powell

"*U*NMARRIED AND PREGNANT" *is synonymous with the image
of "bad girl." Many unmarried mothers-to-be confront
their parents fully aware that the reaction will be one of
overwhelming shame and disappointment, an undermining of
the family's "good" name. Although today increasing numbers
of unmarried mothers are choosing to raise their children, in the
past many families felt that the quickest route back to their quiet
and respectable lives lay in hiding the evidence, while searching
for someone who was willing to remove the embarrassment of
an unwanted child.*

*Facing up to an unwanted pregnancy, often while still a
teenager, is a lonely and testing experience. Sometimes the child
has sprung from a loving relationship, but equally often from a
casual, meaningless one, and occasionally from violence. The
women who decide to tell their parents may receive reactions
ranging from unqualified support to horror and even physical
abuse. The young prospective mother's relationship with her*

*family may erode and, with it, her own sense of self-esteem. The
news was devastating for Rishy Powell and her mother:*

If I could have had the choice of picking the worst news for my
parents, other than murder, it would be that I was pregnant.
Here was a Jewish girl, twenty-one, living at home, and the
baby's father was not Jewish.

I tried to get rid of the baby. A friend of mine knew somebody
who gave some kind of douche. She did it but it didn't work. The
woman said if you went down the stairs on your bottom, you
could jar it. I had to wait for a time when everyone was out, and
then there I was going down the stairs, bumpity bump. Needless
to say, it didn't work. I tried again, but it still didn't work. The
baby was there; it wasn't going to move. So that's when I told
my mother.

We lived above a grocer's shop, and the sitting room faced
College Street. My mother was reading a novel and smoking. We
were alone. I came into the room and said, "Ma, I have something to tell you."

She said, "What is it?" and continued to read.

I said, "I don't think I can tell you while you're reading."

"I can hear you. Go ahead."

I said, "I'm pregnant."

She said, "What? How did it happen? Who was it? Is he
Jewish?"

I said, "I'm pregnant, but don't ask me to marry him because
I won't."

She asked if it was the first time. You see, if it was the first time,
then I was a good girl gone bad. If it was more than once, then I
was a tramp. I said, "What difference does it make? I'm pregnant!"

She got very upset. How could I do this? It was a terrible thing.
She didn't want my father or anyone else to know. Getting up
from the sofa, she said, "How could you do this to me? I thought
you were a good girl."

I said, "I am a good girl. I'll get an abortion. What do you want me to do?"

She said that she didn't want me to get an abortion, to leave it with her and she would work something out. I was really worried about how my mother felt about me.

She spoke to my two aunts. One of my aunts went to the same doctor as I did. She said, "The doctor knows who I am. Don't let him know you're my niece." That's the way it was in those days.

I was going to have the baby and put it up for adoption. I had no choice in the matter. That was my mother's choice. She said it was the best thing for me to do; I would have a better chance of getting married.

For the last three months of my pregnancy I hid in my bedroom. My father never found out. During those months, when my brother and father went to work, I would get out of bed. When they came home, I'd go back to bed. I was able to get away with it because I have Khrone's disease, an inflammation of the intestine. My brother would ask my mother why I was always ill and she would say I had Khrone's.

Rishy Powell's pregnancy arose from a mismatched young relationship, but one that had a degree of positive choice. Sonya Hayes, aged only fifteen and living on her own in a furnished room in Toronto, had an altogether more brutal experience:

One Saturday evening my landlady's daughter, who was nineteen, invited me to come with her and some of her friends to a dance. We went, and I drank alcohol for the first time.

At the dance hall I saw several people I knew from school. There was one boy who was very handsome, and he asked me to dance. Later he walked Yvette and me home. I sat with him on the front steps, then he was in my room and was locking the door. It was Saturday, and everyone was out. My screams went unheard. I begged, but it was over in two minutes and I was still dressed. I had been a virgin. While I was crying and saying I could be pregnant, he said I couldn't be — not after the first time. He said he had to leave and be home before midnight or his mother would be angry.

Twenty-year-old Mary Anne Cohen had met the man of her dreams and had assumed that they would marry. When she learned she was pregnant, however, her expectations were shattered:

When I finally told my boyfriend I was pregnant, I was in for a rude surprise. He told me he no longer loved me, was seeing someone else (all those nights at the library, ha!) and that he would pay my bills but wanted nothing to do with me or the child. I could do whatever I wanted with it. I just wanted to die.

A Christmas card re-established contact with a boy Pat Tyler had met at summer school and gone out with during the autumn. His card rekindled the flame, and her life was changed forever:

It didn't take me long to find out I was pregnant. I even seemed to know before I missed a period. I went to the doctor about a week after I missed my period and sure enough . . . I was shocked and in a state of disbelief because I was young and optimistic that these things would never happen to me — it's the optimism of youth. I was scared, yet secretly very happy that I was becoming a mother. I had fallen very hard for this fellow and really would have preferred that we could have married and I wouldn't have had to face the ultimate. That was very difficult for me.

The father was about my age. He certainly was unprepared to solve my problem by marrying me; he made that quite clear. I could understand that, but I still had to face all the consequences. He tried to come up with a means to abort the child, but I certainly wasn't too keen on that idea. After I told my parents I was pregnant, my stepfather went to his house and had a little bit of a showdown.

In those days being pregnant and unmarried was a tragedy — a serious, serious thing. It was a big responsibility, and there was a stigma attached to it.

Jean Clark's family was not very communicative at the best of times. Finding the right time to tell her parents she was pregnant was not easy:

My father took me out one afternoon to give me a driving lesson. I was sixteen. I said, "Dad, I'm pregnant."

He said, "I don't know what I'll do, but I'll worry a lot," or something like that. I thought, "Thanks a lot." When my dad told my mother she said, "Just get out of here." You know, cover it up.

My boyfriend was the first person in my life who said, "You're really okay," and, of course, I was very attracted to him. He was a kind man and when I told him I was pregnant, he wanted to get married. It was his mother who said no.

Liz Vineberg White had suffered childhood abuse by her mother. It wasn't until she was twenty-four, nine years after relinquishing her own baby, that she learned she herself was adopted:

When I was fifteen I was raped, and my adoptive mother took me to New York and left me in a home there. She never asked what the circumstances were. Someone had hurt me terribly, and I couldn't tell anyone. As soon as she noticed I was pregnant, she started calling me filthy names and within two days she'd taken me away.

I spent the next five and a half months away, with no communication, except with my dad. And then she showed up seven days after my daughter was born with clothes and blankets and undershirts, raving about how beautiful my daughter was, asking me to name her after her grandmother. She told me that I could keep her, and I was just so thrilled. Here was someone who was going to love me regardless, somebody that I could please, maybe.

And then, of course, she dropped the bomb and said, "Well, if you do keep her you can't come back home, nor can you contact any member of the family ever again." And I was only fifteen, so I knew what I had to do. My mother said, "If you've made your decision, then you dress the baby." We took the child out and got in the car. She parked outside the adoption agency and made me go in by myself and physically hand my daughter to a stranger and sign these papers through a veil of tears. I never really saw what I was signing, it was just "Sign here." When I came out I was crying so hard I ran straight into a parking meter. I got into the car, and we drove from New York back to Ohio. Not a word was spoken, not one word.

When we got home I started taking my things out of the car. She said, "Where are you going?"

I said, "Well, to my room."

And she said, "Anyone who gives up their child doesn't deserve to sleep in a bed. You will sleep on the floor in the hall from now on."

Pat Tyler was whisked off to the Ontario countryside to keep her secret intact:

I didn't start to show early; then I was hidden away in the cottage over the summer and tried to rush in and out of the house so I couldn't be seen by the neighbours. In the autumn I was sent to Humewood House, a maternity home. They had a nursery there, but no babies. You weren't allowed to bring your baby back from the hospital. They tried not to be judgemental, but we were definitely outcasts. It made the whole process easier for them because part of conditioning or brainwashing you so that you gave up your child was to have you sequestered off, away from other influences, where you followed the herd — everybody else was giving up their babies, too. I remember one girl started to entertain thoughts about keeping her baby and the social workers just swooped down on her. They really worked on her. Once you were there, the path to giving up your baby was all set up.

Susan Baines was sent to a home for unwed mothers three hundred miles away:

I came from a very religious and strict family background. When my parents found out, my father threatened to shoot my boyfriend on sight, and he would have done it. I was hidden away at home whenever there were visitors. Even my grandmother went to her grave never knowing about my baby.

Sherry Luce hid the fact that she was pregnant, even though she continued at school. Although she stayed at home, she went through her emotional ordeal alone:

I grew up with a mother who thought a library was a great thing and that the greatest thing in life was each of us getting a library card. So when I started to consider adoption I went to the library and found *The Adoption Triangle* and started to read it. They thought I was mad because I couldn't take the book home, and every day I went back to the library to read, and cried and cried and cried.

At this point I was eight months pregnant. Still nobody knew; I never showed. I was in such denial that I never allowed myself to look or be pregnant. I went all the way through until I was about three weeks from my due date before I called a local agency.

When I was growing up, my attitude towards adoption was

that it was the most wonderful thing in the world for those who want to adopt children. I have adopted cousins, and I thought it was nice that, although their own moms didn't want them, Kay and Uncle Frank did. My attitude was that those women who gave their children up didn't care and didn't want them. The thought of an adoptee ever wanting to know who his birth parent was never even entered my mind.

And then I went to adoption agencies and said, "Place my child for adoption. I'm due in July and I want to know who the people are who will adopt my child."

I was told, "Absolutely not! This is not an option." They said I wasn't mentally balanced if that was what I wanted to do.

When Pat Tyler needed understanding she, too, found there was no one to turn to:

No one could help you. There was also the stigma — you were sentenced to secrecy because there was no understanding for out-of-wedlock pregnancies. It was like it was your own damn fault.

Rishy Powell suffered utter desolation during her pregnancy:

I think that I just felt I was bad and had done a very bad thing, and whatever happened to me was deserved. I deserved all that anguish and pain because I caused all that shame for my family, not what I did to me, but what I did to my mother.

Rose DuPont Moir had been seeing her boyfriend for a year, and they were making plans to marry when she found out she was pregnant:

Unfortunately he was Protestant and I was a Catholic. Although this didn't matter to me it was really important to my mother.

My father had died in 1928 in a drowning accident, and she was the one who looked after us. She was a little General. You couldn't say no to her.

One day I realized I was pregnant, and when she found out he was gone. I was twenty and was three months pregnant when I told her. I was afraid to tell her, and when I did she immediately thought of abortion, but her cousin, who was a doctor, told her that this was illegal. I stood my ground and was determined to have the baby.

The day I went into the hospital I was alone. No one came with me. My boyfriend was nowhere to be seen. I hadn't seen him for months and knew that my mother must have contacted him and, whatever she told him, he was long gone. I don't know how she did it, but I never saw him again. In those days it didn't take much to put the law on to you, and that's what probably happened. Mother used all the wiles she knew, and that was it.

Unlike Rose's boyfriend, David Morrow decided to stand by his girlfriend Wendy. They had known each other for three years when she became pregnant:

She couldn't go home and had to go somewhere before her pregnancy showed. So she came out to Alberta and lived with me in my tiny one-room bachelor apartment in Calgary. It was furnished and it was small, but we managed. Wendy told her parents back in Nova Scotia that she was working for an oil company. I bought her a cheap wedding ring so she would not be embarrassed if someone noticed she was pregnant. We pretended to be married except, to my everlasting shame, when we ran into someone I knew, in which case we pretended not to know each other.

Just before Thanksgiving, on October 7, 1966, Wendy told me that it was time, and I took her to the hospital. In those days even husbands couldn't be present at the birth, but I visited Wendy in the hospital and saw our little daughter several times. She was a fine, healthy little girl.

The adoption was arranged while Wendy was in hospital. I was an articled clerk at the time, not yet called to the bar. I had this strange notion that the "disgrace" of having a child out of wedlock could ruin my career. So (and this is something else which will be to my everlasting shame) I asked Wendy to put down another name when giving the particulars of our daughter's parents. When I took Wendy home from the hospital the baby stayed there. I have never seen her since.

The moment of birth, usually a joyous occasion celebrated by family and friends, is often a time of sadness and regret for the unmarried mother. Filled with apprehension and despair, she knows she will have to give up her child into the waiting arms of others.

Rishy Powell's labour began while her father and brother were at work and, astonishingly, were still unaware of her condition:

My mother didn't want me to be seen getting into the cab, so I got one a block away. I was in labour. Here I was, by myself, going up the stairs to the hospital, carrying my suitcase. My mother couldn't come with me. I didn't blame her; she didn't know what to do. I blamed myself; I'd done a terrible thing. I went into Emergency, and they treated me like a piece of garbage.

Walking up the stairs to the hospital I could feel the sharpness of the pain getting stronger. My suitcase seemed to be getting heavier, and I felt so alone. From the time I filled out the form at the hospital as an unwed mother, they treated me with disgust. I lay for hours in the emergency section of the Doctors' Hospital, in labour with no medication. The nurse who was looking after me only looked after my cigarettes. She kept coming in to borrow one and managed to take two or three every time. By morning I had none left. She also told me I was getting what I deserved, being an unwed mother. I hated that nurse with a passion.

In contrast, the staff at the hospital in eastern Ontario who cared for Rose DuPont Moir were much more understanding:

The staff in the hospital were wonderful to me, and after I gave birth to a little girl I would go down to the nursery and look at her every day. I didn't stay in hospital too long and was soon about to leave with my little girl. I phoned my mother, who had never been in to see me, to tell her I was coming home. It was Easter Sunday so I nicknamed my daughter "Bunny."

Jean Clark was still a schoolgirl when she found herself in hospital about to deliver her child. After meeting the social worker she was sure that the best thing she could do for her baby was to relinquish her. Certainly she could not rely on any help from her parents:

My mother was waiting for us to grow up and leave home so that they could split up. There was just no consideration. For my little girl it was the best decision.

Pat Tyler was convinced that it would be impossible for her to give up her baby.

I can remember asking my social worker, who was unmarried with no children, if she knew of any homes I could go to with my baby and work for room and board, but she said no. I couldn't think of any other way because there was no welfare. There weren't daycare centres in those days, and if you weren't married, who would babysit for you? If I had been on my own with a roof over my head and a bank account, I might have seen things a bit differently. But with no resources, and being still at school, it was an impossible task to keep my baby.

We had to go to the Out Patient clinics at one of two hospitals. We were treated differently in that we were not allowed to have our own family doctors take care of us. In a way we were guinea pigs because the Out Patient clinics and the unmarried mothers were subjected to streams of junior doctors, which was humiliating. The maternity home was run in a military style and with a strict timetable — wake up at a certain time, turn down your sheets, make your bed in a military fashion.

Once I had actually come to grips with the pregnancy, and then when I began to recognize what I was going to have to do — give up my baby — I cried every night. This was my firstborn baby; I loved my baby. Every time I saw my social worker I cried. I could hardly communicate with her; I couldn't even talk. It was just horrendous.

My son's due date was October 26, and he was born on the 27th. My blood pressure went up about two weeks before he was born, so they induced me. The irony of it is that there was a high frequency of high blood pressure among unmarried mothers who were going to give their children up for adoption. I went through the labour in silence, alone. It was not common practice to phone the parents. You went off to the hospital alone.

The driving force that helped Melanie Tabor, an eighteen-year-old Maritimer, to survive her emotional trauma was the positive feeling she had about adoption:

When David was born, I gave him a beautiful blanket I had been knitting, with his birth date in the corner. I took pictures of him, which I carry to this day.

2

Promise You'll Take Care of My Baby

I would look down into his huge,
innocent eyes and try to explain to him
why I was going to let other people
raise him and love him.

Christina Pfenghanssl

THE TEMPTATION for an unmarried mother to keep her child
against the advice of others is great. This tiny spark that
grew within her is part of her physical being. Surely she has
the right to decide what should happen to her own infant.

In the past the pressures to relinquish her baby to adoption
were enormous. Social workers and parents often convince an
ambivalent mother that adoption is the best way to show her
love for her child, that adoption is best for the child's welfare.
Although the link between Alexis Roberts and her infant was
severed, the magic of that relationship stays with her to this day:

I will never, never forget the warmth I felt when the doctor laid
my son on my stomach. It was a very special kind of warmth.
Although I went on to have three more children, I never quite
felt the warmth I had with my firstborn. With each child born
to me it was always my first that I cried for. Please don't

misunderstand me, I love all my children, but my first was different.

I was allowed to hold my son once. He was perfect. When I went to the nursery the day I left the hospital, they wouldn't let me see him. When they turned me away I died a thousand deaths. I will never forget the pain, the tears, the feelings of destitution as I left the hospital on that cold day in January. It was the first and only time in my life that I begged God to let me die. If I couldn't have my baby, I didn't feel I could go on. I was sick, lonely, hurt, devastated — and alone, completely alone. I didn't have one visitor. It was simply expected that I would have the baby and go on with my life as if nothing had happened to me. The social worker told me that I would forget the baby and that I would have other children, that my other children would then take the place of this one. You know what I say to that? Bullshit!

The young mother may fantasize circumstances in which she is able to raise her child, but reality must eventually intervene. The hospital scene may play itself over and over in her mind for years, as she remembers it as the most critical decision of her life. For Rishy Powell (née Katzman), the recollection of those days in a Toronto hospital is still crystal clear:

A nurse came up to me after I had had the baby and told me I had a beautiful, blond, blue-eyed baby boy. One of the other nurses heard her and reprimanded her for telling me. "You're not supposed to tell her what she had! That baby's being adopted."

The baby was taken away after he was born, but the next day I went to the ward where the babies were, and I asked to see the Katzman baby. Actually they weren't supposed to show him to me, but they did. Just as she showed me the baby, another nurse came out from nowhere and said, "She can't see the baby! That baby's up for adoption and she's not supposed to see him." That picture of my baby has stayed in my mind all these years — thinking I had a blond, blue-eyed son somewhere.

I did a lot of crying in the hospital, and the lawyer wanted me to hand the baby over to the adoptive parents, but I couldn't do it. I said if I saw him or held him, they wouldn't get the baby. So they made an exception.

Christina Pfenghanssl kept her ordeal in a Calgary hospital an absolute secret:

I took great care naming my son Jonathan, after a person I greatly admired and Mark from the Bible. I gave him every feed, pulling the curtains around us and pretending we were alone. I would look down into his huge, innocent eyes and try to explain to him why I was going to let other people raise him and love him. And when I spoke to him he really looked as if he understood, and when I cried and my tears fell on him he just stared at me so trustingly.

There were four women in our room and I remember hearing one say something about what a cold person I was, feeding my child and then giving him away. They had no idea of the pain and determination it took for me to do what was right, for me to ensure that my child had two parents who loved him and wanted him. But one of my nurses knew, and she slipped a photograph of him under my pillow. I cherish it to this day.

The day I left my son my social worker walked me past the nursery one more time, to make sure I knew what I was doing. It was the hardest thing I had to do. I signed the papers and left my son to what I pray was a happy future.

When Mary Anne Cohen went into labour, her boyfriend and his new girlfriend were the ones who dropped her off at the hospital:

I was totally alone.

The labour and delivery were a nightmare because I was totally unprepared. My child was delivered with forceps after a sixteen-hour labour on April 9, 1968 at 7:57 a.m. The sun was rising through the mists of the Paterson Falls, but I saw only darkness and the sick green of institutional walls. I didn't see my son until the next day. Twenty-four hours after the birth I was moved to the psychiatric floor for "observation," because some doctor thought I might be suicidal! I was not allowed to see my son again in the hospital, and was threatened by a doctor with the state mental hospital if I "made trouble." Needless to say, I did not.

A social worker came to visit Jean Clark in the hospital and advised her against seeing her baby or holding her:

But I made regular visits down to the nursery. Anyway, after she was born the social worker came in and made me realize the impact of what I was doing, made me realize how final it was and told me that I had no rights and that I would never see her again and that was all, that was it.

Those who thought they knew best made all the decisions for Patricia Robins. Her family and doctor in British Columbia had assured her that adoption was the right alternative:

I was twenty years old, but unmarried. I had told no one that I had been raped. I didn't see my son until he was about three days old, after much crying. Oh, he was beautiful. I had known all along that I had wanted to keep this baby.

Fifteen-year-old Sonya Hayes's mother contacted the Children's Aid Society in Toronto, who suggested she be placed in a home as a mother's helper while she was carrying her child. Despite the isolation from friends, she found there was always someone special close by:

I talked to my baby while she was safe within me, and I know she knew I loved her. I was very sick and two weeks overdue when I entered the hospital to be induced to have her. After twenty-six hours I had a beautiful little girl.

I held her, fed her, bonded with her and loved her. I was given no options for help. On the sixth day after her birth my mother and the social worker came to the hospital and gave me a choice: either I sign adoption papers or my mother had the right to do it. I pleaded and cried, but those were the facts. I remember thinking if I was ever going to be able to forgive my mother for not helping me then I couldn't let her sign. I signed the papers.

They let me stay in the hospital for another two days, and we shared some more time together. On the last day there was a ritual one must go through. I was taken to a room while my mother waited outside — she had warned me not to cause a scene. The nurse brought in my baby, Carol, and passed her to my social worker who passed her to me. They say babies don't smile at eight days old, but mine did, and it seemed to me she was saying, "It's okay, I understand and I'll find you later."

Brenda Hobbs and her boyfriend were too young to take care of an infant when she became pregnant, so Brenda was sent to a home for unmarried mothers. She says that the decision to adopt was not hers, but that "I suppose I was simply grateful that the predicament had been taken out of my hands and a decision was made for me."

I remember the very first time they brought Gabriel Dawn to me. First I fed her, burped her, hugged and kissed her, then took off her blanket, nightie and nappy and counted every finger and toe to make sure she was perfect! Dawn was a happy baby and didn't fuss. I talked to her in the low, cooing tones mothers use, telling her how sorry I was that we had only seven days to know each other before I had to leave, but that I would love her always and would be waiting with open arms whenever she found she needed me. This is how it had to be; after all, I was only fifteen.

Then it was day seven and time to go home. My mother and her cousin came to pick me up. I was happy to be able to fit into my clothes and that, at last, I would be back home, but that meant leaving Dawn behind. I gave Dawn her first feed early that morning and said goodbye. As my mother wheeled me out of my room, she asked if I wanted to look at her one more time, but I knew if I did I wouldn't be able to tear myself away from her. As we were leaving, a nurse said, "Her baby! She can't leave without her baby!" My mother wheeled me very quickly into the lift and away from the nursery. I didn't cry, at least outwardly. I just felt frozen in time, empty inside — a feeling that has never gone away.

Doreen Lamb became pregnant by a married man. She was twenty-six at the time, and spent the last part of her pregnancy at an unmarried mothers' home:

I gave Paula up. I was very, very unsure at the time and, looking back, I realize I didn't have enough counselling. My parents supported me. They were elderly, and I had other brothers and sisters. I remember ringing up once from Putney and saying that I didn't want to give her up. They said, "No, no, don't. If you don't want to, just bring her home." But I thought, no, I can't. It's such a stigma with all the neighbours and everybody. And also I was thinking of the child. I had nothing to give her.

The shame that Rishy Powell felt remained with her as she left the hospital:

I took a cab to a block before our apartment, in case someone should see me. I walked the block and then up the two flights of stairs. I felt so empty and cold. I still had pains in my stomach. The doctor said it was the womb going back into place.

My baby was born February 24, 1954. My mother became pregnant with my kid sister in March and gave birth that November. I resented my sister at first, and then I realized why. My mother was allowed to keep her baby.

When I came home I felt weightless. I felt so empty. Part of me was gone, part of me that I'd carried for nine months. It was gone, and I had to get on with my life. From that moment on, everything I felt, all my emotions, were suppressed. I think I got stuck, at the age of twenty-one, with a lot of my emotions. From that time on, I had a lot of headaches, a lot of backaches, depression, and I never knew where it was coming from.

Every birthday, every Christmas and even insignificant daily events can jog a birth mother's memory, forcing those like Alexis Roberts to relive the moment of parting:

I never forgot him. I cried myself to sleep for I don't know how long. I was a very angry young lady after this experience. No one talked to me. It was believed that if you didn't talk about it that it would be easier to forget. My parents never brought up the subject.

Birthdays are always painful. I have a special statue that my youngest brother gave me for Christmas one year. It has a light in it. Every December 26, my son's birthday, I keep the light on for twenty-four hours as a symbol of my love for him.

Shortly after she learned she was pregnant, everyone tried to convince fifteen-year-old Rosemary Schade that adoption was the answer:

It was the hardest decision of my life. I wanted to keep her so badly, but my nerves were gone, my hair was falling out in clumps and I was so emotionally weak at her birth. As soon as I saw her I knew I had to keep her.

Well, my doctor convinced us that to give her up would be the right thing to do. I guess I still know in my own heart that I was doing the right thing. I wanted to finish school and to have a career. I thought I would give Marion every chance in life by giving her a family and all the things I couldn't provide.

I have hurt so much for so long it's as if the hurt is a part of my being. For over ten years I was unable to even talk about her. I held it all inside me. I still have difficulty talking about her, but I know it is best that I do. I want to cry.

It's as if a piece of my life is missing. Every day I wonder about Marion. Who she is, what she is doing, where she is. Does she hate me or resent me for not fighting harder to keep her? I have had this pain for twenty-four years, and I can tell you it doesn't go away. Sitting here writing all this down has brought up so many painful memories. I cry as I write. . . .

Almost immediately after she had relinquished her baby, Patricia Robins made an effort to get him back:

I went to Legal Aid. I was so sure I would get him back. I was given visiting rights, two hours every week. I would pick him up at the social worker's. There were two court dates that I remember. I did everything I was asked to do: arranged for a sitter while working, bought baby furniture, baby clothes, and life insurance with my son as beneficiary. So sure was I that I would get him, I turned down a visit in January, the one before my last court date. I thought I would make a good impression by not missing that one day at work. I was wrong. The judge said I wasn't emotionally equipped to raise a child, and my lawyer did nothing to defend me. It was a nightmare.

I was told I could apply again in six months. By that time my son would be learning to talk and recognize people. I wanted him to have a family, not to be sitting in foster care for months at a time. There was no guarantee that I would be able to take him home at the end of that six months. I told the judge that it would be better for him if he was adopted right away.

I had a breakdown; I couldn't cope. My baby was gone. I was told I wouldn't have been a good mother.

Ironically, the next year I married. One year later, on February 24, 1969, I lost my husband in a motor accident and on February 25 my daughter was born. I raised my daughter on my own. I found out after my husband's death that he had gone to Social Services to try to get my son back for me.

Even though I became pregnant through undesirable means, I loved that baby from the minute I knew he was growing inside me. I love my daughter very much, but she can never replace my son. I had been a virgin before that rape.

What was it like to give up my child? It's not just "what *was*" but "what *is*." It still hurts a great deal. I still cry. On Boxing Day 1966, on my last visit, I took photos. I have one with me at all times. Stanley Charles will never be forgotten.

As the years have passed, Pat Kellogg Friedman has begun to accept some of the responsibility for the action that made such a difference to her life:

I was eighteen when I gave up my son. Probably old enough to have raised him if that was acceptable to society and parents. It wasn't a joyous occasion. Social workers were involved, and certainly my parents' first words were, "You'll give it up!" Abortion wasn't the issue.

And so the decision was made. For twenty years I didn't think about it, and when I finally did think about it, it was with a tremendous amount of pain. I wanted to be able to say that giving up the baby had not been my decision. But after I met my son and began to talk to people about the issue, I would find myself saying, "The decision was made for me."

At some point I realized that I really was in on the decision, and I think that's when I really started to grow. I finally started to get on with my life and to shed some of the anger.

When her mother and minister made plans for Linda Tennant to go to a home for unmarried mothers and then give up her child for adoption, she felt mostly relieved that someone had brought some control into her life:

I came to realize that placing my son for adoption was the only sensible thing to do. It was the only way I could feel sure he would have the benefit of everything a child deserves: a loving mother and father and financial security. I wanted more for him than I knew that I, as an eighteen-year-old, could provide. I have never regretted my decision.

It may be of interest to you to know that in the years following his birth I had three abortions. The abortions were far easier to handle at the time. It was easier than going through a pregnancy, walking away from the hospital knowing I would never see my son again and going through the rest of my life always thinking about him. But I feel guilty and remorseful about the abortions; whereas the adoption makes me feel good. I did something great for someone else!

These are hardly the sentiments of birth father Robin Wise, who was seventeen and living in a small town in Ontario's cottage country when his fifteen-year-old girlfriend became pregnant. He still recalls with bitterness how their young lives were controlled by those anxious to maintain certain social standards:

My father was a Commander in the navy, and her father was wealthy. Believe it or not, nobody but the two of us knew about it until right at the end. September 14 was when the balloon went up. We were just two terrified teenagers.

I knew she was pregnant right away, but it was something we hoped would go away. She got no medical attention, nothing.

She went into labour on September 14, 1963. I wasn't allowed to know anything. I went to her house, and her mother answered the door in a rage and said, "I don't know what to say to you." They physically dragged me in but wouldn't tell me anything except that I was to do what I was told and keep my mouth shut. I was told to leave, not to speak to anybody and to come back when I was summoned, which I did. I didn't say anything to anybody; I was petrified.

About a week later I was summoned, and when I got to her house the family was there, plus a lawyer and a secretary. They made me sit down at the typewriter and type a letter saying that I approved of adoption for the baby, but I wouldn't sign it. I thought they were going to work me over. Then they told me I was bloody lucky they weren't going to have me thrown in prison because she was under-age. My parents still didn't know. So, I signed away whatever rights I may have had. The legal secretary dictated a letter, which I typed on an old Underwood manual typewriter. I can remember the big gold Underwood label on it. It said I was in favour of adoption and it was the only thing that could be done. I wouldn't sign it until they'd pressured me sufficiently, which they did.

I wasn't allowed to see her in the hospital. After I signed the letter I was told I was to attend the house, just as I always had done on Sunday afternoons, and that a bunch of girls she went to school with would be there. They had been told she'd had appendicitis. We had a frightfully proper tea. I was ushered into the drawing room and told where to sit and to be very proper in front of all these girls. Absolutely nothing was ever mentioned about the baby. Appendicitis yes; baby no.

I went to the house every Sunday and kept up appearances

and was ushered into the drawing room. I'd take a book with me and sit there for hours and read. Nobody spoke to me, and when they thought it was appropriate they kicked me out. I went there for weeks, and I was terrified. I really thought they were either going to beat me up or put me in prison.

It wasn't until about two months later that my father found out, by accident, from the village doctor, who just happened to mention to him that my young lady had had a bit of a problem. My parents asked me about it, and my mother got very upset and asked where the infant was. I said I didn't know.

I had very Victorian parents, and this was not the kind of thing I could discuss with them. My mother said, "Why didn't you tell me? He could have been brought here." She was mortified. She tried to talk to the mother's parents but they wouldn't acknowledge anything.

The decision to raise or relinquish her baby was also taken away from Rose DuPont Moir, but in a different way. She fully intended to raise her daughter, brought her home from the hospital and had returned to work leaving her baby in her mother's care during the day:

My daughter was born on April 12, 1936. It was during the Depression, but we seemed to be coming out of it, and I thought things would get better, but they didn't. One day my mother went for a walk with my baby and came back alone. She had given her away, and I never found her again. It ruined my life and left me with an emptiness, a void.

I thought everything was going along fine. The trouble was that Mother was always doing things without my permission. One day I had said I'd like to have the baby christened. Next thing I know, Mother has taken the baby for a walk and come back saying, "The baby's been christened." She said, "I picked the name you had, Barbara Joyce, and added the priest's name, Raymond, because I like him so much."

She was always taking the baby to the park for a walk. One day when the baby was almost a year old and I had just come back from work and was making the supper, Mum wanted to take her for a walk. This day she had her all dressed up in a beautiful little salmon-coloured outfit, with a bonnet and little white shoes. She looked just like a little doll. Mother walked out, and I waved to them and said, "Don't be too long, we're going to have supper."

When she came back the pram was empty. I said, "Where's Bunny?"

She said, "She isn't coming back."

I said, "But, Mother, she's my baby."

"Not anymore," she said. "I gave her away."

I haven't been able to find my baby since.

Judith Kizell-Brans, the director of Parent Finders in Ottawa, has found that a lot of women are never able to grieve for their loss. As a birth mother herself, she remembers it being like a death with no body:

You may not have been allowed to see your child, and you may not even know if you had a live birth. They used to put the babies in a separate section of the nursery so that the birth mothers wouldn't be able to see them.

My social worker said I was the best mother in the world; I was loving, I was caring; until I went into court and signed the papers. Then I became this terrible woman. How could I possibly give up a child? Society viewed me as this woman who had sex outside marriage, who had given up a child. How can you give up your own flesh and blood? So I was condemned. Had I changed my mind I would have moved from a loving, caring mother to a selfish woman who thought only of herself and who wouldn't be able to provide her child with anything.

How can any woman give up her child? It is probably the worst thing anybody ever has to do. Most of the birth mothers didn't make that decision on their own. They were influenced by social workers, by parents, by friends, by their boyfriend — each had a lot to do with it. It was an embarrassment for the young girl to be pregnant, and the family usually said, "You have two choices: either you're out and we don't support you or you get rid of the baby and we'll give you a roof over your head."

Brenda Hobbs has been searching for her child for twenty-two years:

My broken spirit has been haunted by memories, my heart hollow and aching. I have looked from babies in carriages to toddlers to adolescents and teenagers, and now to young women, wondering if it is my daughter I'm looking at. Always searching. I am convinced it is this experience that has prevented me from settling down. From letting go and experiencing joy, for the fear that, wherever and however I find it, it will once again be taken from me. I know that it would not allow me to leave the country and take roots elsewhere, for what if some day Dawn should beckon me and I'm not here?

For Rishy Powell the son she relinquished always remained a question without an answer:

How can you miss something you've never owned? But deep inside of me a large piece was missing.

After Joan Mackintosh had her baby daughter taken from her she had only one reaction:

I wept for days, weeks, months. . . .

When I was coerced into giving up my beautiful baby, I turned my back on God, believing hell was here on earth and there was no heaven. I became quite neurotic in the years following my trauma. Although I did have a baby in 1960 and another in 1962, the children were difficult and highly strung, like me, and still are tense. I blame myself: I produced them while in an unstable, neurotic state.

I was prescribed tranquillizers and to this day am addicted to sleeping pills, although I am overcoming them. In short, I believe my life was ruined by being forced to give away my precious offspring, although I have forgiven those who forced the issue.

Sixteen years after giving up her son, Alexis Roberts gave birth to her last child. She was struck by the similarities between them, and an uneasiness began to haunt her:

I remember keeping my new son very, very close to me all the time. I wanted him within eye range during his waking hours. I wouldn't leave him alone. I had a strange feeling that I was somehow going to lose him. When he was six weeks old, I went to the baby's room, bent over his crib and said, "Don't worry, no one will ever take you from me." Deep down I was sure I would lose him.

I have now registered with a local adoption disclosure registry and desperately live for the day that my son will search me out.

By the time her son was five, Margaret King was married and had two more sons:

... but he remained on my mind and bound to my heart. I again sought legal counsel. I was told I had a very good chance of regaining custody of my son. But I had to choose. Was I being selfish? What would I do to my child, tearing him away from the only family he knew? What would I do to the people who had raised him this far? I had been told that they were a professional couple, quite comfortable, and that he was well provided for. My decision? I decided it was better I live with the pain rather than hurt him and his new parents. But I vowed that when he was old enough to make his own choices, I would find him.

Still feeling upset at the unrelenting pressure exerted upon her to give up her child for adoption, Amanda Tilton has since confronted social workers about their tactics:

There are now indications that adoption is not always so idyllic for the adopted as birth mothers were led to believe. Although some social workers admit privately the extent to which they counselled adoption, to my knowledge there has been no public apology for the way birth mothers were misled and very little public acknowledgement that there was pressure in favour of adoption and that those unmarried parents who would not agree to adoption had to face hostility from the social services.

This means, then, that the social service workers who once believed in adoptions so very much are not taking responsibility for their own actions, but instead they're dumping all the responsibility on us birth parents. By their silence they have led interested parties to think that surrendering a child was entirely the birth mother's wish.

Susan Bishop wrote the following letter to her son Wayne Paul, expressing her anguish over her loss. She still feels the empty space left by the son she once held and has been searching for him since he turned eighteen. She says, "Three years have passed and every time the phone rings, I hope it will be him."

As I write this, tears are in my eyes, as they are whenever I speak about you. It is still hard after twenty-one years to accept the fact that I might never meet you as an adult. The day I gave you up I told you I would find you somehow, somewhere. It was the hardest decision I have ever made in my life. Let me go back a bit.

When I found out I was pregnant, I felt my world crumble. I was frightened and didn't know which way to turn. Abortion was not an option, giving birth was. I knew from the beginning that I couldn't possibly raise a child and was determined to make sure that the child was brought up in a home with two people who loved each other and could give him the life I never had. My parents were alcoholics, and my brothers and sister were not happy. I was afraid I wouldn't be a good mother, even though I began to love you. I had many talks with my social worker, and he supported any decision I made. It was a decision made out of love, Wayne. I cared too much for the child inside me to give him only one parent.

When you were born, I insisted that I take care of you for the five days I was in hospital. I dressed you, fed you and counted your fingers and toes. Your little tufts of auburn hair stuck straight up, and you seemed a happy little boy. The day I left, I went into the nursery and held you close to my heart and cried because I wasn't taking you with me. I was so worried that you wouldn't be okay and that you would hate me for giving you up.

Three weeks after you were born, I talked the social worker into taking me to your foster home. It was definitely against regulations, but he did it anyway. Your foster mother had made you a pair of blue booties and a sweater. I held you so tight you cried. I left happy because you were healthy and your foster mother seemed to love you.

When you were adopted I tried to get as much information as I could about your new parents, but they wouldn't tell me very much. They only said that you all seemed to love each other and that you were all happy.

Twenty-one years later I still think about you. The pain of leaving you is still there. I miss you, my child, and even though

I gave you up, not a day has gone by when you haven't been in my thoughts. I would like to know who you are and how you are, if you are happy and healthy. Please try to find me.

When Evelyn Evans was twelve, her mother left the family, leaving Evelyn to care for her younger brother and two sisters in Kingston, Ontario. She subsequently ran away and got pregnant twice. She had to relinquish both babies, even though she made a valiant effort to care for her second daughter. Her story continues:

I went downhill and started drinking heavily, running with a rough crowd, thinking I was "enjoying" life. I met the father of my second child, and we became an item again. Of course I became pregnant. I made up my mind that I was going to keep this child no matter what. The father, of course, went on his merry way.

I had my baby and went on welfare. We had a two-room apartment which we called home. My life at last had some meaning. My daily existence revolved around my child. Welfare money didn't go far, and my child ate before I did. My health suffered, and it reached a point where I was hospitalized. My cousin took my daughter into her home, supposedly until I was well enough to care for her again.

I had Laurie Anne for three and a half years, but crisis set in again. Partly due to my own behaviour upon regaining health and partly because of my cousin's opinions, my child was taken away from me. My cousin told the Children's Aid society that I had abandoned my daughter.

I was twenty-two years old, had lost my three daughters, had very low self-esteem and felt that life was not worth living. I must admit that I contemplated suicide, but thanks to a girlfriend, I turned my life around.

When I was twenty-four I met a man and married. We were happy and working to buy a house. He put a great deal of pressure on me to have children, but to be honest, I felt as though I did not deserve to bring any more children into this world. We were married for eleven years, and then we divorced. I respected the fact that he wanted children, and when I finally told him why I couldn't have any more, he said, "How could you ever give up a child?" Needless to say, that hurt very much.

Upon filing for divorce, I moved away, hopefully to start anew and maybe forget some of the hurt and pain. But the pain has never subsided. Each day I think of my daughters and wonder how they are. They are also in my prayers each night.

Kim Watson is another birth mother who surrendered her child when the child was a few years old. Kim was nineteen when she put her two-year-old daughter up for adoption in Nova Scotia; although she was married to her child's father, she had just left him:

I was struggling on sixty-five dollars a week from my job and day care ate up twenty-two dollars of my take-home pay. I received only forty dollars a month support from the father, who wanted nothing to do with either of us. I was having a very hard time coping, both financially and emotionally, and was becoming increasingly concerned about my own and my daughter's physical and emotional well-being. My family was marginally supportive, but the attitude was that I had made my bed and I must sleep in it.

I loved my little girl very much (I still do). I thought I was going to go crazy with worry, fear, guilt (because I found myself resenting the fact that my life seemed to be over before it had even started) and very afraid that sooner or later I was going to take it out on my daughter. I was so afraid that I wasn't doing right by her. I talked to the only support people I could find at the time — several ministers and the "friendly staff" at the Children's Aid society. They were very persuasive that I should give her up in order to "let her have a decent life." I still wonder why they seemed so keen on this; perhaps it was obvious to them that I was headed for trouble, I don't know.

But it was ultimately my decision, and I let her go. I took her to a foster home, along with my social worker, and I left her there. I will never forget the look on her face when she realized I was leaving her there. I will never be able to understand or forgive myself for having it in me to do this. I have paid every day since with guilt and shame, and this experience has scarred me for life.

I had to go to court a few weeks after this, along with the father, who was all for giving her up and "wiping the slate clean" and starting anew. Coincidentally, it also meant he didn't have to pay any more child support. The bitterness I felt against the father is nothing compared to the guilt I feel for having done what I did.

Yet in many ways it saved my life. Giving up my daughter was really a sacrifice in order to save my own life, to get my own life back. I went back to school, travelled, went to university and now own my own business. The experience helped in one way — whenever I found myself thinking I couldn't do something I would just think of all I'd been through and think, No, I can't waste this chance. Giving up my daughter gave me the chance to do something with my life. I have to go on and do it, and not fail. It made me keep trying.

When I contrast what my life would undoubtedly have been had I kept my daughter, I have to say that in many respects I probably made the right choice. My biggest fear is wondering how her life has turned out. I worry that she may have been abused or may have been scarred for life by having been left by her mother. It's hard to explain, but she wasn't unwanted — I just wasn't able to care for her and myself at the same time. I made a selfish decision, and I have to live with that. It's very hard. It's hard to look in the mirror and realize I'm the kind of person who could give up her child.

My family doctor was the only other person who supported my decision. When I told him what I'd done, he said, "You did the right thing; you broke the circle. Now you both have a chance for a good life." I've had to keep reminding myself of this throughout the past twenty years.

I pray that my daughter has had the kind of life I tried to give her, that I wanted for her when I gave her up. I wish I could have had pictures of her as she was growing up and could have maintained a relationship with her, at least to be assured that she was okay. This not knowing just haunts me. I did receive nonidentifying information on what happened in the year after I gave her up. It said she was terrified of getting into a car — that she might be "left" again. That just broke my heart.

After I remarried and my second daughter was born, I had cancer of the cervix, so I contacted the Children's Aid Society. My thought was not to try to get in touch with my birth daughter (I was made to understand at the time of the adoption that this would be impossible), but to provide some information about family health in case she ever had need for it. I never wanted to disturb, disrupt or intrude upon her life in any way; I gave up all rights to that twenty years ago. But that doesn't mean I wouldn't be happy beyond belief if she ever tried to contact me. Even if she just wanted to tell me how much she hated me for what I did, I would still like to have contact. I registered with the Adoption Disclosure Agency, and if she ever comes looking she will be able to find me. I will wait all my life hoping for that.

Dr. Zellig Bach, a New Jersey psychologist who has conducted extensive studies on adoption, confirms that many birth mothers suffer "psychological amputation." If the greatest tragedy that one can imagine is the death of a child, then for the birth mother who has given up her child the grief is comparable. Mary Anne Cohen's experience confirms this:

I went home and my son went to foster care. I became severely depressed. My heart was broken, my breasts kept dripping milk in spite of the numerous "dry-up" injections, and everyone acted as if nothing was wrong, as if I had become clinically depressed for no reason at all. The fact that I had lost my lover and my son was never addressed. I was filled with antidepressant drugs and urged by the doctor to date others, get on with my life, forget I'd had a child.

I became even more distraught and my son remained in an unknown foster home. I was allowed to visit him about once a month at the agency but was never allowed to meet the foster mother or to know where he was living. The agency's counselling continued to be geared towards surrender and towards how he was becoming unadoptable as he got older.

The small amount of self-esteem I had left was systematically destroyed by the year of therapy and counselling while my son was in foster care. I finally surrendered when he was a little over a year old. I have no clear memory of seeing him for the last time. Perhaps it was too painful to remember, and my mind repressed it. But I never protested, just did what I was told like a good little zombie. If I had made waves, perhaps I could have regained my child, but I never did. I never tried. I just did what I thought others wanted me to do. I say this with the deepest shame. My lack of courage cost me my child. I will live with the consequences forever.

The day I signed the surrender papers was the day a part of me died. I remember what I was wearing. I remember the other people in the court. I remember my father cried. But neither he nor anyone else tried to stop me, tried to save me. My boyfriend was long gone, and everyone else just let me slide down that long, dark road to hell, where a judge handed me a pen and said, "Stick it in your hand and sign," and I did, and died. In my mind that day was black and red, ink and blood. I saw no future for myself, only oblivion. I was not actively suicidal but wouldn't have much cared if I just happened to die.

Alan Burnell, a counsellor at the Post-Adoption Centre in London, England, says that society's negative attitude towards birth mothers may have moderated slightly but still remains:

In some ways it's gone full circle. The stigma used to be about having intercourse before marriage and being a loose woman and all that. Now the stigma is not about that but about the fact that you've actually given your child away. That's what people are vilified for. Even in the more open climate now, it's quite difficult for a woman who's given up a child for adoption to publicly acknowledge it because she'll still take a lot of flak, not for being loose but for being heartless.

It's a big issue. Young teenagers, how much choice do they have, really? Who's putting the pressure on them to give up their child? They're making a contract as a fifteen-year-old — to give up a child — when actually they can't vote or anything else. It's a major life decision being made by somebody who's still a minor and who probably still hasn't got the intellectual ability to think about the long-term consequences. So you often see women in their twenties who have given up a child when they were a schoolgirl very remorseful and bitter about it. And often they suffer from postpartum depression when they have a subsequent child in a marriage because all the suppressed feelings from five or ten years ago come to the fore.

3

Into New
and Loving Arms

*My beautiful baby daughter came to me
on one cold but sunny wintry day, only
nine days old.*

Pam Moncrieff

*T*HE NEWBORN BABY'S STAY *in his or her mother's arms has
been a temporary one. Now the child must move on, and
new parents are ready to welcome him. These adoptive
parents will love and care for this child and steer him through
the many difficulties that all children must overcome before they
reach maturity.*

*Michael Blugerman, executive director of the Children's
Resource and Consultation Centre in Toronto, is a leader in the
field of adoption. For twenty years he has been helping families
and feels strongly that adoptive parents hardly receive the rec-
ognition they deserve for the devotion and love they have so
freely given:*

The adoptive parents don't have an equal corner of what is
known as the adoptive triangle. From the moment they find that
they have an infertility problem, it's very hard for them to get
sympathy. Most people are pretty unsympathetic. They're told

they must be selfish. If God had intended them to have children, they'd have had children.

Even good adopting parents sometimes feel that they are not entitled to raise this child. Their blessing is someone else's loss. They had more advantages than the birth mother, and for this reason they are raising someone else's child. In the infertility process these people have been poked and prodded; then they come to adopt, and they need to be assessed, scrutinized, screened and approved.

There are many who are anxious to fulfil lives they are convinced are empty without children. Unable in many cases to have children of their own, they seek to care and nurture the children born to others. Catherine Moore and her husband had been interested in having a family for a long time but a medical problem had denied them the opportunity:

I had a burst appendix when I was a child. About fifty percent of people in that situation have a lot of internal damage, and I'm one of them. We decided to look for a child for private adoption because the numbers of children available were really low by the time we got into this in earnest.

We had known they planned to place our daughter with us about six weeks before her birth. The birth mother had been offered a number of families who met her criteria. She decided what kind of family she was looking for, and she selected us. At that time people didn't often meet the birth parents, so we just waited and hoped. We'd had other opportunities fall through just before placement, fortunately not just after. That's part of what you have to put up with.

I remember the day we went up to pick Janet up because we were very excited. We got to the small town too early and went to McDonald's for breakfast. In the little hospital we took pictures, and the staff took pictures of us. Everyone was checking us out because she'd been there nine days. At the end of the weekend, after taking photographs of this whole glorious thing, we discovered there was no film in the camera! I decided that, if that was the worst thing I did to her, we were in luck.

We didn't meet her birth mother. The more I got to know my daughter the more I wished we had.

I don't remember the trip home at all. Everyone in our circle had been very well prepared, and they were very supportive. I couldn't believe the outpouring of affection to her and to us.

Janet's birth mother had signed a consent to relinquish custody for the purpose of adoption, and we had to wait twenty-one days until her rights expired. It didn't interfere with our feelings for Janet at all, in fact we had thought it would be like a stone off our backs when the deadline passed. But it was a nonevent. We were just so enthralled with her that it didn't bother us at all.

We picked her up nine days after she was born because the birth mother can sign a consent to relinquish custody eight days after delivery. Janet's birth mother felt that if she could do two things, first, leave the hospital without the child and, secondly, sign the consent to relinquish, that everything — this is a strange expression, but they are her words — would be all right. I don't know how all right things were for her, although I do know that she's not felt differently about her decision. We were not required, nor was it in our minds, to continue corresponding with her, but as time passed, John and I got a greater and greater sense of what she had done both for Janet and for us in making that decision. I thought about her, particularly around Janet's birthday.

Catherine was so happy with the adoption of Janet that she was determined to adopt another child:

My daughter and I were sitting at the table. I was reading off the names of licensees around Ontario, and I came to one, Jenny

Painter, and she said, "That's a pretty name." So I wrote to the woman, and she wrote back saying that she'd like to meet us and we should bring Janet. We met Jenny, and I don't think she was particularly impressed with John and me, but she liked Janet. You could tell that Janet understood about herself and her circumstances, that adoption was the way our family had been built, even though she was just about four.

Jenny called us three weeks later. A couple had already had a baby, and he was a couple of days old. They had gone through all Jenny's files and chosen us. We were just blown away. My husband was at work, and his office door was closed because he was firing someone. Jenny was desperate to get hold of us, and she finally said to his administrator, "You should tell him it's urgent. I want to speak to him about his son." Well, this woman knew he didn't have one, so she interrupted the meeting.

Then we went down and met Thomas's birth parents, and they explained to us why they had made the decision they had made. They had asked us to bring Janet, but we didn't feel we could. It just seemed too sudden and too uncertain. But we took down Janet's life book, which is a book of pictures, and shared that with them, and I think that made the meeting pretty smooth. We came home and told Janet that she was going to be a sister, and then the next day I got on the train and went back and looked after Thomas in the hospital. On Monday night we got the call; on Tuesday we went down and met the birth parents; on Wednesday I started to look after Thomas; on Friday afternoon we had a permit from the ministry to bring him home. It's a shock to the system.

The difference from the placement five years earlier was that we met the birth family; we were required to correspond with them and send them a certain number of pictures. It's funny, I felt so much more comfortable about a lot of things. I felt a greater sense of entitlement. It's now an open adoption. It was finalized as a semi-open adoption, one in which you've had a meeting with the birth parents but you have no direct contact; you contact through an intermediary.

Clara Will is the executive director of the Mental Health Centre in Toronto and is one of Canada's leading authorities on children with behavioural problems. Clara and her husband Leslie now have two adopted girls. She recalls the adoption of their first baby:

We didn't know the birth mother. We just had certain information given to us by the Children's Aid. Just a little bit of family history, a little bit about the conditions of the birth, why the mother had decided to put her daughter up for adoption, that kind of thing. It was very clear that she was a bright baby. Everybody wanted her. And our social worker was fighting for us. The situation at birth wasn't because the mother didn't want her; the mother was young and unmarried.

More than anything in the world, Sabina Erlich and her husband Allan wanted children:

We tried for eight years to have children. I registered with every doctor that I knew. I went to visit homes for unmarried mothers — there were no babies. I made plans to go abroad, which didn't materialize. I had doctors and lawyers looking from Vancouver right over to Prince Edward Island. We were covering the country.

I was in New York with Allan — he was doing a show there — and I got a message to call my friend. I called Toronto, and she said, "Your son has been born!"

I said, "I'll be back in three hours." I had packed and caught a taxi to the airport in ten minutes.

It's so incredibly emotional because you don't know whether or not the birth mother will change her mind. Even though the mother has said for nine months that she has to give this child up for adoption, the Children's Aid Society will place that child in the mother's arms, and the bonding will take place. I was told I could pick him up on the morning of the fourth day. I had a very, very difficult time because the mother did, in fact, change her mind.

When I picked up the baby I had eight other mothers waiting to receive him with me because I felt so insecure. My sister and my friends came — it was like a receiving line. My son was premature — he was only five pounds. I brought a receiving blanket, and they put him in it, put him in my arms, and I thought, There isn't a baby in my arms. There's no weight. I thought, because I'd miscarried so many times, This is some terrible joke. But I looked, and there he was!

So I came home with him, and the eight other mothers stayed with me for the first forty-eight hours. I was so nervous because I didn't have the nine months' preparation, even though I was a nurse and had worked in the intensive care ward! I never saw the birth mother.

I knew I had the baby for twenty-one days, because the mother had the right to change her mind. We passed that, but then we ran into problems. The mother phoned the doctor after two months and said she wanted her baby back. So I got a call saying, "You will be given eight hours' notice to return the baby." My husband and I talked the whole night and agreed that under no circumstances would he be separated from us. My husband said, "I will leave the house and my job, and we will kidnap the child and go to South America! We are a family. There is no way he's going to be separated from us."

This single mother had no support from the father of the child; she had no support from her family; she was unemployed. The lawyer told her what steps had to be taken to get him back, and she did not fulfil the steps in the required time. But I wasn't to know that until three months were up. In the third month we started to breathe more easily.

Six months later Sacha officially became mine. Growing up with Sacha was absolutely marvellous. He was the easiest, most wonderful baby. I wanted very much to have a brother for him, and two years later, I adopted my son Andrew. That was a lot easier because the birth mother and birth father knew, one hundred percent, that they couldn't bring up the child. They wanted a sibling for Andrew, which I had; they wanted a mother who was a nurse, which I was; they wanted a good economic background, which we had; and they wanted adoption preferably out of the province, and I was offering that.

I knew about Andrew two months before he was born. They flew me out to interview me. The birth mother left it to the grandparents and a very close family friend. I lived with them for four days, and they got to know me. They asked me many, many questions about what kind of life Andrew would have. All the papers were signed.

I flew out when he was born and was able to take him out of the province on the eleventh day. There was a snowstorm that night, and they cancelled the plane. I said, "Right. I'll take a taxi ninety miles to another airport. I'm not chancing staying and waiting for the weather to turn. I want my son home."

Pam Moncrieff still remembers the day she welcomed a new member into the family:

My beautiful baby daughter came to me one cold but sunny wintry day in March 1951, only nine days old. My husband, a bag of nerves over the event, had run out of cigarettes and had dashed out to buy some. No sooner was he out of sight than a large black car pulled up and two social workers from Children's Aid came out carrying the baby. Once in the warmth of the house, they pulled back the blanket covering that precious face, and I swear the little smile that glorious babe gave me was as if she was saying, "Here I am, I'm yours."

From that day on she has been nothing but joy to me, but I never ceased to be saddened by the fact that somewhere out in the world was a mother who would never know what a lovely child she had brought into the world and what an artistically talented one. What she has missed having to give away that precious child.

Of course, not all children are adopted at birth. Some adoptive parents, like actor Roy Rogers and his wife Dale Evans, welcome older children into their families:

Dale and I were in Britain playing concerts and stuff like that. We got into Edinburgh, and a chief constable there wanted us to go out to this orphanage that he had an interest in, in his spare time. When we got there, there was this little girl about eleven years old who was going to entertain us. She sang the little song, "Will You Buy My Pretty Flower?" Both Dale and I sat there, tears rolling down our cheeks. When she finished I asked the guy if she was available for adoption. Yes, he thought she might be. So we said we'd like to bring her over to the States for a summer vacation. Well, she came, and when it was time to go, of course, she didn't want to go and we didn't want her to leave. Anyway, we called Willie, the chief constable, and asked if there was any possible way that we could get around the strict Scottish adoption laws. He said that we could become her foster parents, so we did that, and she's been one of ours ever since.

When Patricia Atkinson adopted her daughter she had no idea that the birth mother lived in the same town near Toronto:

We were probably five minutes from each other. Because we met at the social worker's home in another town, she naturally assumed we lived there. I didn't know whether to sell the house and pack up and leave or what to do. I was afraid to take the baby anywhere. For the whole of the first year I dressed her like a boy most of the time. I showed a distinct preference for unisex clothing!

It's awkward because you owe everything to this person, the birth mother. You are so grateful to her, you almost love her intensely, even though you don't know her that well, because she's given you something you could never have without her help. You're incredibly grateful and petrified of her at the same time.

Right from the beginning the ground rules are very clear. You're raising a child who's both yours and someone else's. I see it as no different from raising a child of divorce. I don't think visits are appropriate for young adoptees, I think it's confusing.

What's amazing to me is how many ridiculous comments are made. I've had people congratulate me for doing a wonderful thing for humanity. As if I was saving the world. Isn't it ridiculous, because I consider myself the lucky one. I've had other people say to me, "How does it feel to raise someone else's child?" They simply don't understand.

Nowadays, it is the norm for adoptive parents to tell their children they are adopted. For some parents it is difficult to decide how and when to broach the subject and how much to say. Patricia Fenton started very early:

Even before she would understand the meaning of the word, even when she was an infant, we'd perhaps use the word in a song or I'd say, "I'm glad we adopted you," at bedtimes and snuggle time. Adoption has always been part of her life. She's just finished grade three, and she did a project this year on adoption.

You have to acknowledge that they have another family, another background. Ever since Katie was about five she's asked about her birth family. She can't understand why we don't visit the family. Not too long ago she said she was going to write a letter to the government because she said, "Whoever made that rule that you have to be eighteen before you can do any search, well, I just don't like that." I think she'll do a search, and I hope I'll be around to be a part of that. I really think we're looking at a trend towards greater openness in adoption.

Clara Will and her husband Leslie both agreed they would be quite open about their daughters' adoptions from the very beginning:

I think it was because I had worked with a lot of children who were foster children and children who were adopted. So it wasn't a new concept for me. I guess I've always believed very strongly that every person has the right to know their history. Right from the beginning both Leslie and I felt that although this was our child and we were her parents, it didn't mean that she shouldn't have as much knowledge as she could get about her own birth history.

Telling her two adopted children presented no problem for Sabina Erlich:

I told them they were adopted from the moment I had them. When they were infants I was talking to them about it, and I continued to talk so that by the time they were a year or a year and a half, they had heard the story a hundred times. They were very comfortable with it. I said those were the happiest days of my life and they had changed my life immeasurably. I need them; they needed me. We were meant for each other. I said I was the unhappiest mother-to-be for nine years. It was wonderful, in fact, that I didn't conceive because then I wouldn't have had them.

I've already told them that I know where to find both birth mothers. I don't know quite where to find my older son's birth father. I will help them both to search. I will go with them and make every effort to reunite them, if they so wish.

Catherine Moore had no concerns about telling her child about her adoption since she was convinced that it was important to be honest and to maintain a link with the birth mother:

Every year, starting that first year, I wrote her a letter, talking about Janet's year, because I assume that at eighteen Janet will want to search. She may or may not, but I want everything to be as smooth as possible for her and her birth mother. The first year I sent it off to the social worker with a note saying that if she heard from Janet's birth mother she could send this on, but she didn't hear from her. By the second year I was really starting to wonder, and the social worker suggested she call her and see whether she was interested in hearing, and she really was. In the letter the second or third year, I told her I was hoping to find another child to adopt. I know how she thinks about Janet and about us because an opportunity came up through her family. She contacted the social worker, and they tried to arrange for that child to be placed with us. The baby was born quite prematurely, so the mother hadn't had a lot of counselling, and in the end, it was a really unfortunate set of circumstances and it didn't work out. That's how I know that what I do by writing to her means something to her, even though she's not able to communicate back to us.

Janet Bishop's daughter knows that she is adopted and very much loved:

She has a book with photographs of her birth mother and members of that family. She has regular contact with her half sister and, when the time comes, she will be told the truth about her adoption as kindly and compassionately as we can. If she wants to see her birth mother then I hope to have the strength to help her make any arrangements that may be necessary. She knows how much she was wanted and that she's loved very much — probably more than some children who live with their natural birth parents — by both my husband and me, and our respective families and friends.

Ruby E. Miller and her husband Ron adopted Amanda at birth, and two years later Melanie was born into the family. When Amanda was four or five she began to ask questions:

It bothered her in some ways because other children asked her, "Are you really adopted?" Our two children are so different. One is a redhead and one has dark brown hair, one is olive-skinned and the other very fair. People would ask, "Which one of the two is adopted?" and it would irk Amanda.

From the age of twelve, she read articles and books about adoption. She brought home a book from the library and read it, and all she said was, "Mum, read this because some day I'm going to have to do the exact same thing."

I took the book and read it. When I finished reading it I said, "I think we should talk about this." So we sat down and talked about birth parents, reunion and so on.

From then on it was a slow process. Sometimes we talked about it every day, sometimes it got very emotional because she got so upset she could hardly contain herself. We, of course, got upset, not at her, because of her problem, but because we were completely limited, we couldn't do a thing, we couldn't provide the information she needed.

On the morning of her fifteenth birthday she unwrapped her last present, and she looked down at it and started to cry and said, "I can't stand it any longer." We couldn't stand it any longer either. I phoned Parent Finders that very morning because I knew, without a doubt, that I had to do something and I had to do it quickly. She was so upset.

Joan Longworth Parkinson is an adoptive mother of two children. She feels that when the subject of adoption is discussed her side of the story is ignored:

We feel hurt that the government, after saying that the files would remain locked, has now seen to it that they are not. This could cause a lot of heartache for women who thought their past was buried. Perhaps the people in their lives now know nothing of these children.

As for myself, I sometimes feel when watching TV programs on this subject that my life's work of loving and caring for my adoptive children counts for very little, as it has no intrigue or glamour.

Although Margaret Wood remembers the joy she felt when, after waiting three long years, she and her husband were able to adopt her daughter Tammy, she feels the advice she received from the social worker was not helpful. Margaret believes that this led directly to Tammy's subsequent behavioural problems and difficulties with relationships:

The social workers instructed us that we should tell our child as soon as she was able to talk that she had been chosen by us rather than born to us. So it was from the beginning that our daughter, like so many adoptees of the time, was deprived of the feeling that she was truly one of the family. You and I know otherwise, but to Tammy, no matter how glowing and wonderful the story was made to be, the one thing that came through in her mind was that she was inferior, unworthy and rejected by the one person who should have loved her above all else — her birth mother.

By the time Tammy was three years old, my beautiful sweet little girl had turned away from her grandmother and me. If we tried to hug her she would struggle. If we tried to give her a kiss, she would turn away. A gift could be taken with indifference or discarded with hostility. On the other hand, her father and grandfather were allowed to come close and enjoy her affection. It became clear that she did not associate the story of her birth with men. The story that we had told Tammy was of her birth mother, who, with love and concern, had given up her child so that she could have all the wonderful things that we could give her.

This child has had all the things that others could only dream about. Big brothers to look out for her, her own horses to ride, swimming, music and dancing lessons, wonderful holidays, loads of toys and a large family that has always supported her and loved her as its own. Still her feelings of low self-worth turned her into a brooding, evil-tongued and hurtful individual. She has shown all the traits of a troubled adopted child. In our ignorance we thought that somehow we had failed her. Tammy could not say goodbye to anyone. She hoarded everything, lied and stole. More recently she has made herself as unattractive as possible by ignoring personal hygiene, putting on a great deal of weight and dressing in a masculine fashion. Our counsellor has told us that her reasons for doing this are to protect herself from a close relationship with others. If someone likes her, she might in turn like them and expose herself to the fear of rejection.

Throughout her childhood Tammy has had psychiatric help, but until now the system has failed us. The best thing that has happened to us was our recent trip to Children's Aid. At last I see a glimmer of hope. Here I was told for the first time that the reason for my child's hostility towards me is that I represent "mother." The wall that she has built between us was to protect herself from becoming too close to me and making herself vulnerable to the fear of rejection.

Although Tammy has our support in searching out her birth mother, it is doubtful that she will. Like countless others the fear of being rejected a second time is too great. How I wish that we had never told her about her adoption. At least we could have waited until she was old enough and strong enough to understand. Our counsellor now tells us that people are encouraged to withhold this knowledge from their children until after the child has enjoyed a few years of untroubled childhood. Authorities also agree that adoption is unnatural, except in the case of death of the birth parents, and birth mothers are encouraged to keep their babies in the light of the problems of these children.

I will continue to stand by my daughter despite the weariness and hardships our relationship holds for me. If only she could see that I am her real mother, not the woman who carried her for only nine months. Believe me, it takes a lot of love to stand by a child for this long and take all the abuse, in exchange for the few fleeting moments when she forgets. The sweet, loving, talented and intelligent being escapes now and then from beneath the tormented individual she has become. I hope that one day my daughter will pull through and come to terms with herself and her relationships.

Adoptive parents may view their child's curiosity about his or her birth family as a comment on their adequacy as parents. What if that youngster eventually decides to search for his or her birth parents? Will there be enough love to go around?

Janet Bishop and her husband adopted their daughter when she was four years old, and her reaction to a possible search in the future is typical of many:

Can you understand what it is to live with the knowledge that the child you love and cherish as your own may one day decide to go and find her birth mother and you could lose her?

Many parents suppress their anxieties and let matters take their course, but some may take drastic action in their opposition to any retracing of the past. Harriet Perchaluk says that when someone offered to help her daughter trace her roots, Harriet put her foot down:

When I found out about it I just called her and told her, Fine, go right ahead, but the minute she found her mother I would make out a new will and exclude her. Well, I can tell you that was the last we ever heard about the subject.

4

Growing Up Adopted

Who the hell am I?
James A. Michener

*H*AVING LEFT *the arms of his mother, the adoptee is about to make his way into the lives of those genetically unrelated to him, into a home where a family will take and treat him as if he were their own.*

Life in this new home will probably be like that of any child, but with one major difference. Regardless of how they came to be with their new families, many adoptees will eventually need to know who they are and where they came from. They have, after all, lost the person who played the most significant role in the earliest moments of their lives. The British researcher H. J. Sants has termed this sense of being cut off from one's roots "genealogical bewilderment."

How and when that distinction is revealed to them matters enormously, and there is not always a "right" way or a "right" time to do it. Today some adoptive parents find that a good way to help a child share feelings and thoughts about adoption is to create a life book — the child's own chronicle of birth, adoption and life with the adoptive family.

Christopher Sterling was adopted in Montreal just six months after his birth. He was four years old when he discovered the truth:

I was informed about my birth by a nanny who was taking care of me. My adoptive parents were on vacation. The way I was informed really had a very profound and disturbing effect on my life because she said, "You know, your parents aren't yours really. They don't really belong to you." She informed me that I was adopted, and I immediately made a lot of decisions that my parents were never going to come home; that actually they had left me with this woman. It got the whole thing off on the wrong foot. Then I began to have a lot of psychological dysfunctions; I had recurring nightmares of the same sort of thing, of being told this and not knowing how to verify it, being too young to use the phone and not knowing how to get validation or proof. I was an only child, so I didn't have any siblings to discuss it with. So here I was, living alone in a house with a woman who just gave me this information, and that was it.

Jas Wilson was seven years old and, being an inquisitive child, came across some papers in a desk drawer:

I was old enough to read them and understood that something was different about me but not old enough to fully understand everything. My mother found me with these papers, and then both my parents tried to explain to me and my brother about adoption. It was a very hurried explanation, and not all of it was heard by me. All that kept going over in my mind was that my parents weren't my real parents and my brother wasn't my real brother (he was also adopted).

I tried to find out more by asking a school friend about her parents: Was her family like mine? No, they were not. Then I got teased by other children, so much so that I couldn't face going to school anymore. I used to make myself physically ill so I could stay at home. My mother got suspicious and took me to see the headmistress, and the children responsible for the teasing were admonished. Things eventually settled down, but from that day I seemed to grow away from my parents. The thought of any parental contact, like hugs and kisses, repulsed me.

I left home as soon as I could but I couldn't settle. I had to keep moving on. It didn't help when every time I applied for a job I was asked about family medical history. I always had to say I didn't know because I had been adopted. Their replies were always, "Oh, I'm sorry." Then they changed the subject.

It wasn't until I was in my mid-twenties that a friend introduced me to a homeopathic doctor, originally for treatment for a badly damaged ankle. After a few sessions with her all my life history came tumbling out. All the hurt, anger and frustration that I had bottled up for years was finally uncorked. Apparently I had been on a kind of self-destruct course because of that original rejection at birth. I would get myself into relationships that wouldn't work. It was as if I had to be punished, and being constantly rejected was all that I expected from life. I used to get so depressed sometimes and even contemplated suicide on several occasions.

At a certain stage in childhood, it is common for children to fantasize about not being related to their family, as part of the natural process of developing individuality. But for Ann Kirkman, then ten years old, the timing was unfortunate:

An aunt who had been married for ten years and had not conceived had just adopted a baby boy, and my mother felt this was an appropriate time to tell me of my adoption. Unfortunately it was very traumatic for me because it coincided with a time in my life when I had been imagining that I was an adopted child. I can remember weeping and saying that I wanted my mother to be my real mother.

Deep down I always had this feeling that there was something wrong with me; adoption was treated in such a secretive way, as though it was something to be ashamed of. I couldn't bring myself to ask questions about my biological parents for several reasons: I felt guilty because I thought my adoptive mother would feel I didn't love her; I felt shame because I must have done something really bad for someone to give me away, and I didn't want to know what it was. I can remember feeling that I didn't really belong and that no matter what I did it turned out wrong.

In about 1950 or 1951 my parents moved to Leicestershire, and I decided to stay in London. At first I was living in a women's hostel, and then a friend and I moved into a furnished room in Knightsbridge. As time went on, I began to indulge in what I now realize were very self-destructive behaviour patterns. I had no goals, I was drinking a lot, I became sexually active and was ashamed of this, and my self-esteem was very low — not that I would admit any of this at the time, even to myself.

In October 1953 I married a Black GI and moved to Queens, New York. I gave birth to a son, David, in December 1954. The marriage lasted three and a half years. I continued to work and care for my son but was again drinking too much and had very low self-esteem. I married again in October 1961, and I knew it was wrong from the beginning, but I couldn't bring myself to admit to my family and the world that I had made another mistake and also felt that maybe I didn't deserve anything better. I had two children from this marriage and had terrible guilt feelings about Susan's birth because the marriage was a disaster by then and so was I. I stayed in this marriage and buried my feelings until my father died in 1975. At that point I came face-to-face with the reality of my own mortality, and I was in such emotional pain and turmoil that I just couldn't go on the way I was, and I didn't have the tools nor the desire at that point to change it.

As the adoptee gains the realization that his adoptive parents are not his birth parents, it may be the start of a lifetime filled with the need to know about his origins. The discovery can be especially traumatic when postponed. Don Hunkin's mother did not tell him he was adopted until he was twelve years old:

For several years I had entertained thoughts and feelings about not belonging to my family, possibly stimulated by something seen or heard at school. Apparently this experience is common among adoptees. I asked my mother several times if I was adopted, and each time she answered with, "You belong here! Now, will you please stop this nonsense?" Finally she told me the truth.

Although very kind and generous, my mother had martyred herself to my father's alcoholism and my sister's psycho-emotional dependence. I had negligible contact with either my father or sister, and because of my mother's need to support them, I literally spent the first five years of my life alone. My first real experience of playing with others came with my entrance into the school system.

Knowing I was adopted brought relief that the insanity that cursed this family was not mine by blood. For the next year or so I spent hours fantasizing about my "real" parents. They were always fabulously wealthy, extremely intelligent and highly respected by everyone. I was almost immediately welcomed into their lives, where I lived happily, and spoiled, ever after. Dreaming about this other life supported me through some pretty hard times.

Many adoptees report that the news did not come as a complete surprise, even when they discovered it by accident. Arlene Sioui had often wondered why she looked so different from the rest of the family. The answer her mother gave was that she looked like her grandmother. Then one day at her rural Quebec school a friend's disclosure led Arlene to discover the true reason:

This particular morning, Helene came to school with her knapsack bulging at the seams. She looked exhausted and seemed withdrawn. At lunch, when I asked her what was wrong she broke down and told me. She had found out that she and her brother were both adopted. They were told that their parents had died in a car crash. Helene said she hadn't slept all night; she was thinking of the rest of the family. All she kept saying was, "Where are my grandparents, aunts, uncles?" That is when she told me that she had decided to run away in search of her natural family. I tried to explain to her that her adoptive parents loved her and that she had everything. By the time school had ended that day she had gone.

When I went home my mother could see that I was upset. She asked what was wrong, and I just went into hysterics. When I calmed down I told my mother the story and noticed that Mom had tears rolling down her cheeks. Mom asked what I would do in Helene's position. I said I wouldn't run away, that they were the only parents I knew. Mom then said something to me that I will never forget. She said, "I think it's time we had a little talk. When Dad comes home we'll sit down and talk about it."

They started by telling me that now I was fourteen, I was able to understand what they had to say. In my heart I knew exactly what they were going to say, but I never said it. I loved them too much to hurt them.

Paul Patterson had been adopted as an infant and found himself in a home with no other children. Three years later the family adopted a girl:

It always was rather strange because your friends would look like their brothers, sisters or parents, but I didn't look like my parents at all. I always felt different, not a degraded different, but special.

I was always told that I was adopted. I wouldn't have been too happy about it if I'd been told later. I had known my original name as long as I could remember. My parents never kept it a secret, which was good.

I asked a few questions when I was eight or nine, like, "Why was I given up for adoption?" Adoptive parents aren't really told much, and it seems that most adoptees are told pretty much the same thing, that your mother was young and couldn't keep you so she had to give you up. Young in my mind was fifteen or sixteen, which wasn't the fact.

We didn't really get along too well. I left home when I was sixteen. They did a lot of drinking, and I got into a little bit of it myself, and there was a lot of conflict. When there was friction in the family and they'd ask me to do something, a little bird in the back of my mind would say, "You're not my real parents anyway. I'm going to do what I want." It's a cruel attitude to have, I guess, but it's an honest statement.

It's strange because I remember my sister being really curious about her adoption, always asking questions and wanting to do a search. I never asked any questions, never discussed it with them at all. Then last year I just said okay, I wanted to search, and did it. I'm twenty-seven now.

Maureen Dinner was a well-adjusted child living in Kitchener, Ontario, but still she had questions her adoptive parents could not answer. Fortunately, throughout her thirteen-year search, and after she found her mother, her adoptive parents remained supportive and their relationship is as solid as ever:

I have always known I was adopted. My parents always told me this wonderful story of how I was the "chosen" one, that they went to the agency to look at a child, and they fell in love with me at once. I was never teased as a child or made to feel different in any way. I was as much a part of the family as my sister, who was born to them one year after they got me. Oh, my sister would occasionally say, "Well, you're not my real sister anyway," but that was when we were fighting, and don't all siblings say things in anger?

Christopher Sterling never felt comfortable growing up:

I felt out of place because I was a fairly big person and my father was short so I would always hear, "You look so different from your parents." That caused a lot of discomfort.

The tragic thing about the adoptive family was that they were very different from me, physically but also emotionally and psychologically. I had very different drives. They were very English- and Scottish-Canadian, and I feel very Latin. They were thinkers, and I was a feeler all the way along. Feelings didn't work in that family and weren't appreciated.

Whenever I acted up, my adoptive father would bring out his balance sheet on me and show me how much it had cost them to adopt me. As I got older there was a threat that inappropriate behaviour might cause them to disown me. So I always lived under this fear of being disowned and not knowing where to turn.

Steve Tobis of Toronto was brought up as an only child. He was unaware that he was adopted until he got into an argument with his best friend:

I was about ten years old. I remember that day. I was outside playing in the yard with my next-door neighbour, my best friend, when we got into an argument. He came out with the statement "You don't know who you are because you're adopted."

I said, "How do you know I'm adopted?" and he said, "My mother told me."

I got very upset and went into the house and asked my mother if I was adopted. She confirmed that I was and said, "It's better to be adopted because we got to pick the best of the batch." I just let it go at that, and it didn't really bother me.

But for Marie Gee the shock was dreadful:

I didn't know I was adopted until I was twelve years old, and then it was by accident. One day, while I was going through some old trunks in the attic, looking for some clothes to dress up in, I came across some papers that were in French, and I noticed my name on them. As soon as my mother got home from work, I showed them to her and asked what they said. It was then that she told me, much to my surprise, that I was adopted and that I would probably turn out to be like my real mother — a good-for-nothing whore! From that time on, I never felt so unwanted, empty and alone in my whole life.

My relationship with my adoptive parents was pitiful. My mother treated me like Cinderella — a slave to housework in between the beatings I received. My dad was in the navy and was away a lot, and so he was oblivious to the fact that this was going on, and the rest of the time when he was at home he was too drunk to care.

Margaret Allsop was not told she was adopted until she was fourteen, yet she had grown up in the 1930s knowing her birth parents:

My adoptive parents told me who my real parents were. Mother was unmarried, but Father was married to someone else. I had seen both these people before, but I thought she was my Auntie

Betty. I was always taken to see my father playing in the brass band, although we never spoke, and I just stood looking at him.

When I grew up I knew Mother had moved to Blackpool to live. It seemed so very strange, but every time we went to Blackpool we made it a rule to visit her. The one thing that hurt me was that she never admitted she was my mother.

Explaining how their adopted child came to be part of their present family can help adoptive parents reinforce how much the child is loved and needed. Some families, however, are not as successful as others in making the adoptee feel included. Adele Lawrence's family had the additional challenge of there being a birth daughter as well, and their unintentional cruelty only reinforced Adele's feelings of not belonging:

I was seventeen and my sister fourteen when my dad came into the living room with an old picture of himself at fourteen. He sat down beside me to show me and called Nancy over. She sat beside me on the other side, and Dad showed her the picture. Then his parental urge came over him, and he said, pointing to the picture, "See, you have my mouth and chin." My mother came to the doorway then and rather than snapping, "Oh, don't do that in front of Adele," she chipped in with, "Oh, but Ken, she has my eyes." And they were all so pleased with themselves.

Maybe Dad finally noticed me or thought of other treasures to be unearthed in the basement, but he got up and left. My sister leaned over and whispered, "I guess you're just a misfit." I sat there for the rest of the TV show, then announced that I was having a bath and going to bed early. I went into the bathroom, turned on the taps full blast, sank to the floor and sobbed.

Although Steve Tobis had previously asked his parents if he was adopted, he decided to ask again when he was thirteen. With his bar mitzvah now behind him, it was important that he know not only where he was going but where he had come from:

I asked my mother again if I was adopted — I guess I had forgotten she had told me or it didn't take effect — and she said yes. I asked, "Where is my real mother?" And she said, "She's dead; she died having you." I was very upset and, of course, broke into tears. It was a very traumatic day, but everything passed. As I was going through my teenage years, all the times I had problems with girls — breaking up and the typical teenage type of ordeals — I would blame my birth mother for the way I was. I'd be going out with one girl and cheating on her with another girl, getting myself into all kinds of trouble. I'd blame my birth mother and have conversations with myself and say that it was her fault. She was a slut and so was I, and it was her fault. If she had raised me then I wouldn't have been like this. I knew I was born out of wedlock because my adoptive mother had told me that.

I couldn't feel rejected by my birth mother because, as far as I knew, she was dead. Because I thought she'd died in childbirth that excused a lot. If I had known then that she gave me up, it would probably have been worse.

Gordon Henderson rarely heard the word "adoption" when he was growing up. The only time the subject was discussed was when he was having problems at school or feeling bad about himself:

I guess it was her way of trying to cheer me up, by saying, "We picked you out," and wanting to make me feel wanted. I didn't like the word: if it was used on the radio or TV, I would somehow manage to change the station. It was like a red-hot sword in my brain every time I heard that word.

Joe Soll mentioned the word "adoption" when he was seven and asked his adoptive mother where his birth mother was. He was

told she had died in a car accident and that was why he had been
adopted:

She got angry. It was understandable (although my therapist later said to me, "Yes, but you made an understandable request, too"). From that day forward until I was forty-two years old, I never uttered the word "adoption," I never said the word, I wouldn't write it. I ripped up crossword puzzles if that was the answer. If I saw "five letters, to take as one's own," that was the end, I ripped it up, gone.

In my first six years of therapy, which started when I was thirty-six, I wouldn't talk about it. I described to my therapist, when I started, in some esoteric way, why I was there, but I wouldn't say the word, so she had to work it out, which she did. I said, "I'm not able to mention the word, so I'm not talking about it."

She'd say, "Joe, it's bothering you," and I'd say, "Yes, it is. I'm not going to talk about it." I was afraid I would die. Every day of my life the pain was there, and I thought about my birth mother, thought, Who am I? Where am I? I didn't fit in; I felt different; I felt unreal. I still do to some degree.

My relationship with my adoptive parents suffered because they had no clue — and had nowhere to find out because it was fifty-two years ago — about how to treat me, that I had different needs from other kids, that the car-crash story, which was designed to keep me from thinking about my parents, didn't work. I didn't find out the truth about that until I was forty-two, but I thought about it every day. I thought about my mother every day, not my father. Not that I don't want to find him, but that's not the real connection. I couldn't talk about it. I was married twice and didn't tell my wives I was adopted. I don't even think I was afraid of their reaction. I was afraid it would kill me — the pain and the anger.

Yes, I felt I was rejected. Take a seven-year-old who's not

adopted, and Mum goes to the supermarket when the kid's at school and gets killed by a bus. Daddy tells the child when the child comes home. The only conceivable reaction in reality for ninety-nine out of a hundred is: Mummy didn't love me, God didn't love me, Daddy didn't love me or this wouldn't have happened. For seven-year-olds it's black and white — Mummy's not here; she didn't love me. Therefore, I am unlovable. From the story I was told, that would have to be the reaction I had. I didn't feel good about myself.

If you're told your mummy couldn't keep you for whatever reason, basically you're going to feel rejected, because you'll come to understand that somebody made a decision. You can't tell a child anything that makes that okay. If you say, "Your mother loved you so much she gave you up," then you equate being loved with being given up, and every time you fall in love with someone you're going to wait for them to give you away. If you were told she couldn't keep you because she was poor, you say, "So? I would have eaten beans." My belief is that for most people the outcome will be rage and sadness.

Alan Davidson's adoptive mother had never revealed that he was adopted. He found out only by mistake when he was eleven. That shock was to colour the rest of his life:

I overheard a telephone conversation my mother was having with the family minister. I was devastated to learn I was not my parents' real son, that my sister was also adopted and that my brother was their own son. I was upset and very hurt. You should be able to believe and trust your mother. It deeply affects me to this day. I rebelled, played truant and failed my exams.

However, I was now determined to prove to my adoptive parents that I was as good as, or better than, their own son. I did, but at a high cost. My brother and I were no longer pals, we were competitors. My mother and I grew apart. I wouldn't accept her apologies or respond to her, no doubt causing her terrible hurt. This still hurts me very much. The damage was done. We would never allow one another to get close again. The desire to prove I was better continued up until the day my adoptive father passed away, even though my brother had died earlier.

To the best of her knowledge, Liz Vineberg White, from South Carolina, was born in New York. She was adopted and raised in Akron, Ohio, and did not find out that she was adopted until she was twenty-four years old. Her home was not a happy one:

My mother had tried to kill herself twice when I was three and a half, and I found her both times. They sent her to a mental clinic in New York, and my grandmother told me I had been bad, that's why she went away, and because I was bad, she might never come back. Up to that time she'd been a good mother, and I thought I must really be a horrible person if my own mother wanted to die and leave me.

When she came back she was hooked on drugs and very sadistic. At first it was intensely physical — throwing me downstairs, pulling out handfuls of my hair, putting my finger in a gas flame until it bubbled (to teach me not to use the toaster because I might burn my little fingers), locking me out of the house in three feet of snow (because my dad had had the unmitigated gall to take me to the dentist). And then it moved into emotional abuse that continued until two years ago — forty years of intense abuse with virtually no respite.

When I was twenty-four I was having some emotional difficulties and was afraid to take the medication that was prescribed because my mother was a drug addict and I was afraid that I would become one too, because it's an inherited thing. An aunt gave it away by asking when my mother had had her hysterectomy. I said, "Well, she's fifty-four and I'm twenty-four, so she had to be thirty."

My aunt said, "Well, she had it when she was twenty-eight." And that was all she told me, which promptly threw me into a year and a half of amnesia. I would have to take my driver's licence out to give my date of birth or say how old I was or what my name was.

I was really furious because my father's only sister adopted a child and I remember them making such a fuss over her, about her being special and that they had chosen to love her, out of all the other children. I asked my parents, "Are you sure I'm not adopted? I really want to be adopted." "No, you're not adopted." I was really disappointed that I wasn't, when I was a child. But I never could understand why I didn't fit in with the rest of the family, although I looked exactly like my father. To my mind I just didn't fit in; I was marching to a different drummer from everyone else.

As soon as I found out I was adopted I went into a shock period and came out of that with an intense desire to find out where my inner feelings came from — why I liked different things from the rest of the family, why I felt a tremendous kinship with people from Ireland, Scotland and Wales. I wondered why I was the only one in the family who liked dancing and music to the extent that I did. I didn't resent being adopted, but I resented the lie. Honesty would have made a much better relationship.

My mother was very, very abusive, and in order to hang onto my sanity I just had to go and unadopt her. I lost my father in October, and there has been some beauty out of his death in the fact that I've been able to grieve for the child in me that was abused and for all the wrongs. It's pulled that emotion out of me and left me this comfortable, empty space with great expectations of filling it with something good for a change. So much pain and anger, all pent in for twenty-five years.

Born into a Protestant birth family and raised in a Jewish home north of Toronto, the confusion over whether or not she was

adopted has only recently been resolved for Dena Rozen. When
she was quite young her mother did reveal her adopted status, but
she later changed her story:

One day my mother told me a big, big secret — that it was a lie
and that she was really my birth mother. Don't ask me why she
did that. She told me this was a secret and my father wasn't to
know about it. I was a very confused child at that point. I only
understood what I wanted to understand, and if I had any
questions I never asked because it just confused me more. So I
kept pushing it all down inside.

My mother was carrying on a relationship with another man
while she was married to my father. She used to drag me with
her every Sunday afternoon to meet this man. It would always
be in a dark little restaurant with dim lights, and nobody would
be in there. We'd sit in the corner, the three of us. Every Sunday
I would meet him, and I had no idea why. All I remember is that
he would reach into his pocket and give me all his pennies, and
that was like my pay for coming.

Some years later my mother finally told me that this man
was, in fact, my birth father. My parents eventually divorced
and both remarried; my mother married this man who was
supposedly my birth father. He was always told, as well, that
he was my father, and that's why he always stayed in touch
with my mother, because he felt a commitment and responsibility to me. I accepted that and never questioned anything. I
never discussed anything. I just sort of swallowed it and went
on.

About two years ago, out of the blue, my mother made a
comment at the kitchen table. She had asked me to do something
for her and I said no, and she started to cry and said, "Is it
because I'm not your real mother?" And I knew that everything
she'd told me was a lie. And I was really, really angry.

I got in touch with my father, and he said, "Of course you

were adopted. We told you you were adopted. I don't know why your mother lied to you over all these years."

I confronted my mother, and she still insists it's a lie, that my father paid the rabbi and the judges to lie. She believes in her heart, I guess, that I'm hers. She had conceived a few times and lost those babies, and in her eyes I'm the baby that should have been her baby.

I'm dealing with a dead end in trying to find my adoption order. She was given that when I was adopted, but we can't find it. She says it doesn't exist. On the one hand my father is very supportive and wants to help in any way he can, but my mother I can't approach about anything. The man she married, who believed he was my father all these years, still didn't believe the truth until I showed him the letter when I got my nonidentifying information. He's also angry with my mother because she lied. He doesn't want anyone to know I'm adopted, and he says I shouldn't tell anyone I was born Protestant: what will people think?

I've put in a request for a search, and it's going to take five or six years, but I'm prepared to wait however long it takes. It's better that it's slow, so I can think about it each step along the way. If it happened very quickly, I don't know how I would react to it. I think why I feel taking it slowly is better is because somewhere down the road I'm setting myself up for a really big hurt, whether she rejects me if I find her or she doesn't exist. So the slower I get there, the better, maybe.

It was such a deceiving kind of thing that my mother did. Now I'm determined to find out where I came from.

Greeba Girvin-Sisson found out only three years ago, at the age of forty-two, that she was adopted. Her story illustrates the comparative ease with which childless people were able to adopt children in the 1950s.

My birth mother gave me up as soon as I was born, I think. My adoptive mother was classified by her doctor as a paranoid schizophrenic when I was five years old, which I only found out two years ago. She pretended to be married when she adopted me, but in fact she had never married. She told my birth mother that her husband was a solicitor. She told the authorities she was a widow. My adoption certificate says she was a widow. How this ever came about is beyond me, except that my adoptive mother had money. Maybe that made a difference, I don't know.

I grew up with no father, and when I was older started to ask questions like "Where's my father?" only to be told different things: he was a brain surgeon and died in a car crash, he was a murderer and was in an insane asylum, he was a writer and drank himself to death, etc., etc.! Following this explanation was, "Why do you want to know? Aren't I good enough?" and then a great big row, and horrible things would happen. I soon learned not to ask too many questions if I wanted to live to be an adult.

My mother and my grandmother raised me. My grandmother fostered my mother (never adopted her), and I gather my mother must have — maybe because of her illness — given my grandmother a bad time, as Grandma always gave in to Mom and she always got what she wanted. Well, when Mom was about twenty-four she wanted a baby. She wasn't married but kept on about wanting a baby, so Grandma, who had inherited money, went down to the orphanage and adopted a one-year-old girl and then gave it to Mom to raise. She didn't want a one-year-old, she wanted a baby, and never really liked Elizabeth. After a couple of years, Mom went on and on again. This time Grandma said, "You go and find a baby yourself this time, since the one I got wasn't good enough." (You'd think they were buying a dress!)

So Mom made Grandma change her name, as they couldn't

both have the same surname, and Mom added "Mrs." to hers and somehow managed to adopt me. Three years later Grandma tried to adopt me from Mom, as she wanted me to inherit a trust fund. Well, Mom refused to cooperate. After another three years Grandma, who wasn't quite normal either, decided to send Elizabeth back to Social Services as she didn't really like her, neither did Mom, and "anyway Elizabeth had dark hair and didn't look like anyone and was an awful handful, always answering back and stamping her feet." I was six and a half and Elizabeth was nine and a half.

I have no recollection of ever knowing Elizabeth, although I have been told we played together. We were being brought up as sisters. Mom said the nuns came and took Elizabeth away, and that we both screamed and cried and they had to tear us apart.

My life growing up with Mom and Grandma was filled with rows and fighting and abuse. I really don't remember much of my younger years. I think Mom's illness, along with her drinking, made life awful. I was sent only to the best schools. There were never any friends at the house. On looking back it all seems like a big charade. Only the best of everything, but never going anywhere, no holidays, and always so much secretiveness.

When I emigrated to Canada I had to show my birth certificate, which caused a great row and awful goings on when I asked for it. Of course it was an adoption certificate. I tentatively asked why, and it led to another big row. So I left quickly. I was always so scared, even at twenty.

Famous author James A. Michener grew up believing he was the birth son of a Mrs. Michener. At the age of eighteen he found himself facing a first official request for a birth certificate:

I had no birth certificate, no trace of who I was. In those circumstances, what the government will accept is a track record put together by a lawyer, with evidence from churches and schools and people who remember the orphanage and so on. Mine was done twice. They tracked me down to age two years. I was in this little town, and I'd been in this Sunday school and people knew me. The government accepted that's who I was.

Now the question was to give me papers, and they gave me arbitrary papers that said I was the son of this woman and her husband. But her husband had died five years before I was born, so it was a total mess. I don't know what the facts were. I worried about it all weekend, then I decided, to hell with it, I was never going to know and I wasn't going to beat my brains out about it. It was shattering because I'd always assumed I was her son. I was told that I'd been picked up and wasn't a Michener at all. It was terrible because then came the question, "Who the hell am I?"

It looks as though I had left New York, my possible birthplace, at a pretty early point and wound up in this town where Mrs. Michener took in abandoned children. An absolutely wonderful woman. She took us in, and I always lived with other kids. That's maybe my salvation. I was always surrounded by three or four other children. She kept three of us under her wing and got us all through high school. She didn't have a nickel to her name; we lived in poverty. As a child I really had nothing. I never had skates or a wagon or sled or roller skates or anything.

She did sewing for a sweat shop. There was never a man in the house. She did have two lovely sisters, one a marvellous trained nurse and the other a powerful high school teacher, and she had two brothers. She had raised them all. That's how she got into the habit. Their father and mother died early, and she became the head of the family at, I think, about fourteen.

We were Quakers. She read to us every night from Dickens and Thackeray. It was astonishing. Also my two aunts were responsible people. They were a fortification and support.

I never thought about whether she was my mother. None of

us did. I knew there was a difference between me and her son who was older, but we never discussed it with Mrs. Michener, never, right up to her death. There was no reason for it. As far as I was concerned she was my mother and I was fortunate enough to have had a good one. She saw me through high school and watched me get a free scholarship to college. She had more than performed her duties. Unfortunately I'm not sure she was aware of any success I may have had. She had the equivalent of Alzheimer's disease.

Former president Gerald Ford was about one year old when his mother and father divorced. He then moved with his mother to Grand Rapids, Michigan, where she married Gerald Ford, Sr. Young Gerald grew up thinking he was Mr. Ford's birth son:

She went to Grand Rapids because that's where her mother and father lived. She married my adoptive father when I was about three or four years old. I didn't actually know that he was my stepfather until I was about twelve or thirteen.

This never bothered me, not at all, because I was treated by my stepfather as though I was his own son. He had three younger sons, and I was treated well, if not better.

When I was about thirteen, I think it was, my stepfather went to court and instigated proceedings to adopt me and give me the right to use his name. It wasn't an act that changed our relationship, because I was very grateful that he had treated me as evenhandedly as he did his own sons.

As for the sons, my younger brothers, we had a wonderful relationship that we continue to this day, a one-hundred-percent relationship. When my mother and stepfather passed away all four of us were treated identically in their respective wills.

I was so happy with my stepfather that I had no desire to meet my birth father, though I did meet him when I was about sixteen and working in a hamburger shop across from my high school, washing dishes and cooking hamburgers. It was a relatively small place, and a man came in and stood across the room about ten feet from me. He stood there for some time, not identifying himself, not buying lunch or anything, and finally he walked over to me and said, "I'm your father." He then went on to say, "Your name is Leslie King, Jr."

I said something like, "Er, nice meeting you," and he asked if I could have lunch with him. So I asked my boss, who said yes, and I went to lunch with him and his second wife. And after a relatively short lunch he drove me back to the school and dropped me off.

He invited me to come out to Wyoming where he and his wife and two other children were living. I didn't do anything about that for about six years. I'd got a job as a forest ranger working in Yellowstone National Park, and on my way out there to go to work in the summer, I stopped off at his house, stayed the night and then went on to my summer job.

My stepfather gave me a great model to follow: He was a totally self-made man and was successful in small business during the Depression. He taught me and my three younger brothers self-reliance, honesty, dedication to what you believe in and good moral principles. Just a perfect role model.

Unfortunately, neither Gerald Ford's stepfather nor mother lived to see the day he became president of the United States.

The pain of separation is more keenly felt by those who were old enough to remember leaving their birth mother. They often continue to relive the trauma of the parting. Hazel Wright, now seventy years old, clearly recalls the day she was taken away from her mother:

We were taken to the children's shelter. Of course, I didn't know what was going on. My brothers and sisters were taken from my mother. It's the strangest thing. I was only six, but I can remember it as though it were yesterday. I was sitting on my mother's lap, facing forward with my head leaning back into her chest, and her arms were around my waist holding me, because she didn't expect they were going to take me. Of course, I didn't know what was going on.

They told her there was no way she could keep me. She cried and, of course, I cried, and they pried her arms from me and took me away from her and dragged me down the hall to the other part of the children's shelter.

I stayed in the shelter, and one day they called me down to the office. There was a man there, and the person in charge asked me if I would like to go home with this man. I said yes. But all I did was cry, although the man and his wife had a big doll for me. Finally the man said that there was no use crying as my mother was dead and I wouldn't be seeing her again.

Jonathan Savan vividly remembers his adoption; he was almost five when it took place:

In Oscar Wilde's *The Importance of Being Ernest*, the lead character Ernest Worthing, a foundling himself, claims to have been found in a carpet bag in Victoria Station complete with a ticket for Worthing — hence his last name. While I never actually resided in luggage, I do remember assuming many of the characteristics of luggage for a number of years. Being a nonstatus native (Métis) in Canada back in the early fifties was to be lost in a limbo of politics. Which level of government would assume the responsibility for us (there were a few thousand kids who fell into this category) was a question that took a number of years to decide finally. In the interim we were bandied back and forth, like the aforementioned luggage, between various foster homes and orphanages.

I remember certain events before my adoption with remarkable clarity. Over the years I have taken a number of trips through areas where I feel this location might be, with a desire to re-experience these remarkably vivid memories. Obviously some thirty years later, the locale would be unrecognizable now and bear no resemblance to that place in my memories. This I regret because it was here that I remember making my first friends. That, I think, is the key behind my memories — a warmth of feelings stemming from the first cognitive experience of personal acceptance.

On the other hand, it is here where I first learned fear. I remember the house, down to minute details: the green wire fence, the dimpled sides of the single-car garage around the back, the seven stairs up to the storm porch, my "brother" Edward and the dark brown horse-leather strap that hung on the back door. Venture too far, be uncooperative, and the bite of that strap across the flesh on the back of your legs would soon make you regret your behaviour. My perception is that I received this punishment far more frequently than Edward, and that was a constant reminder that I was not really part of the family. I was, to the best of my recollection, treated differently.

It was just before Christmas when the Children's Aid Society called to suggest that my adoptive parents take a look at me, and a meeting was arranged for them to "view" me outside the Christmas windows of a department store.

I have very vague memories of the meeting, nice flashes, comforting. At any rate, I seemed to have passed muster and was later invited to their house for a birthday party — my birthday party. I remember that day vividly but, interestingly enough, almost as an outsider. I have a difficult time understanding why, when I do remember that walk up the driveway to the door, it is always as if I was watching myself from outside. The whole memory dissolves as I arrive at the front door. I rang the doorbell and was greeted by my sister Beth, who promptly stated, "You are my new brother," and then asked, "When are you moving in?" (Those are the exact words; I will never forget them.) As I didn't have a pressing social engagement, I suggested that now might be an appropriate time, and the transaction was thus concluded. So ended David Garfield Somers, and so began David Jonathan Savan.

I have been exceedingly lucky. If one were allowed to select parents on the open market, so to speak, I wouldn't have been able to choose better. My adoptive mother was forty-one when my sister, who is three years my senior, was born, and had already suffered four or five miscarriages. I was four, almost five, when adopted.

In moments of fancy, I wonder how, under different circumstances, David Garfield Somers would have turned out and whether I would like him. Statistically, being a native kid, my chances of being in prison would have exceeded my chances of going to university, my chances of being an alcoholic would have dramatically increased, and a number of other, not so pleasant, opportunities would have been afforded to me.

If there is anything that drives me as a result of being adopted, it is simply that I feel a certain amount of guilt (thankfully of a reasonably passive kind) that I was this fortunate and an obligation to pass on some of that good fortune. Given the lack of social options available for the Canadian native population, adoption opened to me worlds that I would never have imagined. I can't comment on the quality of life that one path affords over the other, because I am ignorant of the deep inner feelings of what it is truly like to be a Canadian native, but I certainly do not regret the life I have. Rather, I feel that I have perhaps been given the tools to help other native kids who don't, or won't, have the opportunities that were given to me through adoption.

I am single now, having recently separated from my wife, and have a son whom I miss terribly. I love kids but, nonetheless, recently had a vasectomy because I feel that, should I become attached again, I would not morally be able to participate in the creation of another child. I would, however, strongly push for adopting a child, perhaps one a bit older than I was, so that I might have the chance to pass on some of the love, caring and opportunities that I inherited through my own adoption.

It is difficult to say how adoption affected me behaviourally. I am so aware of the opportunities it gave me that any complaints I have simply become sour grapes. I would say, however, that the insecurity of being a superfluous child in the first years of my life has dramatically affected my relationships with women. I never really got over the fear of being, if not rejected, then not accepted. That is difficult to deal with, but in my case, being adopted was the first step to curing or ridding myself of those anxieties because I am very aware of the fact that I was chosen. In the blackest moments of my life, that realization will always provide warmth and comfort.

Christopher Sterling's adoptive parents never really embraced him into the family. It seemed he was always looking over his shoulder to find out if he was doing the right thing. And, in most cases, what Christopher did was wrong in the eyes of his father:

An adoptee, if he's an only child, doesn't really have any grounds to stand on. And it's taken years for me to establish that I really do have some rights because that statement was repeated to me many, many times, usually with a balance sheet and other forms in hand. When it came, for instance, to taking a job, my father said, "What do you mean, taking this job? That's not a job appropriate to this family." Again there would be a threat to toe the line or else, and when I was a kid the "or else" meant I got beaten with a stick. I was banished to boarding school at eleven because I was just too unruly and too different. I would guess that if my adoptive parents had talked it over when I was eight and had the freedom of choice to cancel the adoption contract, they would readily have done so. It was a monstrous situation.

There is a funny side to the ending of the story because I went on to become so terrified of all this that I moved as far away as I could and got married as quickly as I could. The only reason I got married, one week after college graduation, was that I didn't want to be at home. I married just to escape this tyranny. So the marriage, of course, didn't last long because it was motivated by altogether the wrong reasons. I was clearly on the rebound from the college sweetheart whom my father had forbidden me.

I became successful in New York City in a field that my father had no notion about, investment banking. My father came to New York and spoke to my boss and said, "How could you ever hire my son?" He seemed to be carrying around this shame about me and even had to share it with people who gave me a job.

In 1972 my father called me into his bedroom; he was fatally ill with emphysema. It was early in the morning and he finally broke down and said, "Christopher, I want you to forgive me for all these years of having mistreated you. For your whole life I've wanted to change you into me. It hasn't been until the last couple of weeks that I've felt I've made a mistake." Tears started rolling down his face, and then I started to cry. He died right there. He really was waiting to say those words, wanting my understanding.

One effect of the ruptured bond between a child and his birth mother can be the fear of further rejection. In Joe Soll's case, he sees his difficulty in relationships with women as being directly attributable to being relinquished by the first woman in his life:

Any time I got close to a woman I was afraid she was going to leave me. So you know what you do then? You go out and pick rejecting women. That's exactly what we do. I've talked about this in my group and said, "How many of you have consistently picked people who have rejected you?" They're looking at me, they're nodding their heads.

I also believe that — men and women alike — as adoptees,

when we get married or take lovers we are looking for our birth mothers. Female adoptees, too, are looking for Mommy. Well, we don't know who Mommy is. Most of us don't know her religion, what she looks like, her talents, so we go out on this search for a mate that's impossible to fulfil because we don't have the mechanism that most people acquire, at about five to seven years of age, of identifying a lot of what we want in our mate. We have this other set of birth parents, and it confuses the whole Oedipal issue. I don't believe it's solved for us the way other people have it solved.

We don't know how to pick. The divorce rate for adoptees is a good bit higher. If one accepts the average of divorce in the U.S. as fifty percent, ours is about sixty-eight percent. I think that's significant and that it's caused partly by our inability to pick and partly because of a fear that they're going to leave.

Judith Kizell-Brans, as an adoptee and a counsellor on adoption issues, has a special insight into what it means to grow up adopted:

We adoptees spend our lives with loss and can accept loss easier than we can gains. Adoptees have a hard time accepting praise, are always waiting for the other foot to fall and often will take an action in order to control a situation, sometimes pushing away someone or something — why would we expect them to want to stay with us? Not knowing where you come from, where you get your strengths and weaknesses, encountering resistance for wanting to discover answers others take for granted and the hushed silence and embarrassment when we announce we are adopted, these are the problems you face as an adoptee.

Everyone has an opinion on adoption and search. Adoption, like sex and bodily functions, is not a topic for polite conversation, it seems. These topics are hushed; we know they happen, but we're not to talk about it. Unfortunately, with adoption, the effects suffered from not talking honestly about the outcomes have caused tremendous hardships for hundreds of thousands of people. It surprises me that we have made tremendous strides in medicine, science and technology and yet we cling to antiquated laws and myths about adoption.

Of course, it is inevitable that not all adoption placements are successful. Anna Battler worked for many years in childcare and came across some very distressed children who were in treatment as a result of adoption breakdown:

Several children come to mind: Judy, who, when I would take her shopping, would look at every woman we passed and say, "That could be my mother. Don't you think she looks like me?" Doug, who, while in an angry outburst, would shriek, "You're my mother. I know it. You just won't tell me. Why do you have to go on hurting me?" And Saul (now incarcerated for murder), who couldn't even admit he had been adopted and felt he had been a great disappointment to his adoptive parents.

The anguish and sorrow of these children affected them in every aspect of their daily lives. While we, as childcare workers, attempted to help them feel good about themselves, the bottom line with the children was always, How can you love me if my own mother didn't? And they all felt they had been the cause of their adoption breakdown — that just proved they truly were unlovable.

5

The Need to Find Me

> *A part of my life had always been
> missing, like a piece in a jigsaw, which I
> needed to find.*
>> Janice Raymen

> *Be happy with what you've got.*
>> Susan Bell

*T*HE NEED TO KNOW ONESELF *is vital to most human beings. The answer to the question "Where do I come from?" can ⟁ provide the key to solving the mystery of where one is going. Discovering family medical history, family personality traits and talents can go a long way towards satisfying an adoptee's need to feel complete, and the phrase "completing the jigsaw" is often heard. Most of the following accounts are by those who have initiated a search for their birth parents. However some adoptees decide to end their searches while still incomplete, and others never begin one. They give their reasons later in this chapter.*

Paul Patterson had many questions before he began his search:

It's hard to have a full opinion on something without all the information. I never resented my birth mother because I knew,

I hoped, that no one would give up their child unless it was a last resort. I've met some adoptees who aren't searching because they feel resentment towards their birth mothers. I never felt resentment in that way, but there was always a kind of emptiness, not knowing who you are. It's really hard to give yourself to somebody else in relationships when you don't even know your full self yet.

I've talked to my sister about searching, but she has no desire at all. I sit down and talk to every adoptee I come in contact with now. A lot of adoptees have no idea that they have access to the nonidentifying information. I think every adoptee should at least get that. It can be very enlightening. When I got mine, that was probably the biggest reason why I continued with my search. The last couple of sentences said that Pat was really, really upset that she had to give me up and that if I ever wanted to meet her, she was willing to meet me; her new husband knew about the whole thing, and he was receptive to it, too. That made a big difference. I had the feeling that I wouldn't want to search and knock on her door and have my mother answer with some angry husband out the back ready to kill me. You're going to disturb someone else's life, although that was not my intention. I was doing this for myself, not to rock the boat. I've heard of a lot of scenarios where adoptees have knocked on the door and the rest of the family is irate. My girlfriend had that problem. People related to her birth father totally denied her existence, and it caused a big uproar in that part of the family.

Karen Kloosterman's decision to search for her birth family was a longstanding one:

My adoptive parents had told me from the beginning that I was adopted, but the meaning of the word had never sunk in until one morning when I was around six years old. I had been looking on top of the cupboards in the kitchen and came across a set of silver baby utensils. I can still remember the shock I received when my adoptive mother told me it was mine and that my "other" mother had given it to me when she gave me up.

Bang! The meaning of the word "adopted" sank in pretty quickly. The thought of this other mother bothered me at first. My main question was Why? Why would someone give up their own child? Even so, I was consumed by an incredible curiosity as to who she was, what she looked like, what her name was. I decided then and there that when I was older I would do everything I could to find her.

I was the only adopted child in my family, with two older brothers and a younger sister. I didn't feel I completely belonged. These people were my family, but they were still not of the same blood, and this really meant a lot to me. I didn't feel I was a whole person, only bits and pieces of one put together. I looked forward to the day I turned eighteen so I could put the pieces of the puzzle together and then be able to get on with my life.

It was hard to be emotionally stable, not knowing who I was, where I came from. The question of who I looked like was uppermost in my mind. When we had family get-togethers there would always be the comparing of family resemblances, and I'd just have to sit there quietly, unable to take part.

Although Janice Raymen did not begin her search until she was forty-two, her reasons for doing so had been with her much longer:

As my search went on, I began to realize my reasons and knew they had always been there, but I had been just too frightened to face up to what I would find and the outcome of it all. I realized that a part of my life had always been missing, like a piece in a jigsaw, which I needed to find.

In 1983 Don Hunkin decided that the time had come for him to find his birth parents, and a good place to start would be Parent Finders:

There were over twenty people at the meeting, most of them looking for birth parents. Many of them said that the love and support of their present families was not enough. Despite their accomplishments they felt unfulfilled without knowing their birth parents. The general atmosphere was one of desperate need.

I felt it would be unfair to conduct my search in the spirit I witnessed that night and vowed not to do so. Putting the search on hold, I embarked on a journey of self-examination to resolve my own neediness. I wanted to meet my birth parents as a fulfilled individual with no demands or expectations. I did, however, follow Parent Finders' advice and put my name into the Adoption Disclosure Registry. If my birth parents had also registered then the ADR could arrange a reunion. They had not.

When Liz Vineberg White set out to search the first thing she did was to ask the authorities to open the records:

They're supposed to give you a copy of the birth certificate, and it wasn't there. When we compared papers the only thing I didn't have was a copy of the relinquishment paper, and out of curiosity and, I assume, a large dose of stubbornness because I don't like people telling me I can't know about myself, I asked to see it, and they finally let me see the paper. My birth mother's handwriting was a direct blend of my youngest daughter's and my own. It was like someone had crept up from behind me and thrown ice water on me.

Some adoptees reach an age where the need to know is vital to their future. It may be that they have found someone they wish to marry, and for the sake of the children they hope to have, it is vital that both partners have a full understanding of any medical problems that may arise between them.

Steve Tobis had no great curiosity about his birth family while he was growing up. It was not until he had children of his own that he felt he needed some specific answers regarding his roots:

I didn't tell my wife I was adopted, and it didn't come up in conversation until our second child was on the way. I called up the agency and asked for some medical information on myself, and they said, "Are you looking for your birth mother?"

I said, "No, she's dead." When they asked me how I knew that I replied, "Because my mother told me," but they said all adoptive mothers told their kids that. They asked whether, if they found a match, they should get in touch with me.

I said, "Sure, why not? But in the meantime, get me medical information; that's what I need." As far as I was concerned there was nobody. End of story.

Sharon Leamy initially wanted to find her biological mother in order to obtain her family medical history. She had endured a difficult pregnancy, suffering from a condition she could have prepared for had she known her genetic susceptibility. Then, after her baby was born, Sharon's motives changed. Like many adoptees, with the arrival of her own child she experienced a new empathy with her birth mother:

When I held my daughter in my arms for the first time, I lost control and cried for over an hour. I couldn't imagine what kind of pain it had caused my birth mother to give me up for adoption. It was then that my reasons for searching for her changed. I now wanted to tell her how much I love her, how my life is the most precious gift I have ever received. I want her to know that I am alive and well. I want to hold her and look into her eyes. I want to see if I look like her (and from whom I got my thunder thighs). Does she love to sing the way I do? And does she knit, sew, bake, swim? Do I have brothers and sisters out there? I have a million questions for her.

Jan Rourke says she does not ever remember not knowing she was adopted, but it was never made an issue, either for her or for her adopted brother. She tells of the decision-making process she went through before finally being able to seek out her background, which, as in Sharon's case, started with a need to know her medical history:

So, you ask, what did inspire the search? I suppose for me there are really two answers. The first is the easy one. It is a simple desire to know one's background. One of the first questions any doctor asks when you set foot in the surgery is for a family medical background. Not knowing can be very frustrating, not to mention potentially dangerous. There was always that basic desire for a sense of personal history to call my own.

More important in my case are the factors that are more difficult to put into words. Some mornings, as I was combing my hair, I would find myself wondering if anyone else in my family went grey at an early age. It would be nice to hear someone tell me I had my grandfather's eyes or my Aunt Kate's nose or my mother's smile.

My search was not inspired by a need to find some sense of identity. I knew then, as I know now, who I am. I am Jan Rourke, the extremely fortunate child of a family who raised me with all the love, affection and concern that any individual could hope for. I never felt I was anything other than my parents' only daughter. At no point did anyone in my family, either immediate or extended, ever make me feel as if I didn't belong. In fact, they sometimes expressed surprise when reminded that I was adopted. It just never occurred to them I was anything but a Rourke.

Still, inside, I knew something else. It was like a jigsaw puzzle of a perfect nature scene, but here and there in the image, mostly around the edges, some of the pieces were missing. It didn't exactly spoil the picture, but, still, it was incomplete. Since my early teens I had the desire to know the answers. I used to tell anyone who would listen that the day I turned eighteen I was going to start on my quest.

I saw my seventeenth birthday as the official beginning of the countdown. Even though I had read books and articles on the subject in the past, I was now *studying* them, hoping to find leads on how to speed my search along. While I didn't get many leads, I did get some additional insight. The stories I read helped me to gain a better perspective on my situation. I had been so enraptured by the thought of meeting my "other family" that the possibility of rejection had never seriously entered my mind. However, as I read of it happening to others, I began to question whether an eighteen-year-old, or at least this eighteen-year-old, was ready for that. I came to the conclusion that I was not. My interest didn't fade, but one might say a cooler head was prevailing.

Within a couple of years I felt that I had prepared myself as much as anyone could for all contingencies. I was finally ready to fill in those missing pieces.

Like Jan, Maureen Dinner had always wanted to know about her birth parents:

. . . my mother, mainly. When I was sixteen and quite rebellious, I went to the Children's Aid Society to find my "real" mother because she had to be better than the one I had. The worker there wisely told me to come back when I was eighteen.

Just before my eighteenth birthday, I did go back to get what information I could. My parents had to sign a consent form for me to receive any information. I remember that day so well, sitting across from the worker, who had a manilla file on her desk with all my family information in it — and I couldn't have it. She told me nonidentifying information, things like height, weight, colour of hair, interests, hobbies, musical abilities and the circumstances behind my relinquishment. I asked her for it in writing, as it was a lot to remember. I got a two-and-a-half-page history. I carried that around with me everywhere. It was the only connection I had.

A few years later I joined Parent Finders in Toronto and learned how to search for my family. My searching went in waves. I can't say that I searched for thirteen years, but on and off I did, and it was almost always on my mind. Not that I was obsessed with the idea of finding her, because I could have done a lot sooner than I did. But when the search got close, I kind of backed off a bit. My desire to search increased with each child I had (I have three).

Many adoptees say their desire to search for their birth parents increased with the arrival of their own children. This is what happened for Lois Mandel of Thornhill, Ontario, although the spur to search originated with an earlier rite of passage, her marriage:

Just before my wedding, my mother came to me with all her documents and said, "Look, they're still alive. I just didn't want to tell you, I didn't think you were ready. Whatever you do, I'm behind you a hundred percent."

Actually it wasn't such a big surprise. That's when the desire to find my birth mother started. Then it became imperative after my daughter was born. From the minute she was born I couldn't take my eyes off her because I was afraid somebody was going to walk off with her. I thought, What if somebody were to come into my room and steal my child? Or what if I had to give this child up? The culmination was the incident in the nursery.

When I went to pick up my daughter from the nursery, there was another cot right next to hers. There was a little teddy bear in there and a little note taped on it. It said, "To whom it may concern: Please tell my baby girl how much I loved her, how much I wanted to keep her, but I couldn't. I feel she's better off and she'll have a better life. I want her to know that I loved her."

I think I cried for three days! Once I had that empathy for my birth mother, I couldn't turn back.

Adoptees often give their main reason for searching as an over-whelming curiosity about their origins and the desire to know more about the circumstance of their adoption. For Christopher Berri-man, this began suddenly when he was fifteen or sixteen years old:

I experienced sporadic periods of total distraction. I had spells in which I was obsessed with finding my birth parents. I endured many sleepless nights. I imagined every conceivable scenario as to the circumstances in which I was conceived and given up for adoption. I'd always hoped that my mother hadn't nonchalantly given me away and that she had thought about me over the years.

Jamie Boswell was adopted into a family of four, all infants from the Catholic Charities of Boston:

I always knew I was adopted and always knew I wanted to search. I fantasized that my birth mother had long, blonde hair, was a totally beautiful, successful, blue-eyed woman. I'd always had fantasies like this, but my adoptive mother didn't mind and had no problem with it at all.

I got my nonidentifying information at seventeen and found

out that my mother, Ellen, had given me up when she was twenty-three, which rather blew the fantasy that she was fifteen or sixteen. But I'm still convinced that she had to give me up. When I was eighteen I petitioned the court to open my records and was turned down. Then I petitioned again when I was twenty-two or twenty-three and again was turned down. It depends on the judge you get a lot of times. They said they had to maintain my birth mother's privacy and make sure my adoptive parents didn't get hurt.

When I petitioned the court the second time, my older sister, who's quite flamboyant, ran up and stood next to the judge. She put her arm around him because I was losing my temper and I was yelling in the courthouse. He was ready to throw me in prison or something. She looked down and saw "Haley Murray" in the file. Then we asked a clerk there to get us a first name and the address of where she was in 1965. She did that, which was against the law. So we knew that her name was Laura Ellen Murray. We went through birth certificates, death certificates, through everything, but couldn't find anything. I did most of the search myself.

Before Gordon Henderson embarked upon his search in Alberta, he had to come to terms with the possibility that he might not like what he found:

I thought, No one else is going to help me, I am responsible for doing something about my own life. I will make that search, I will accept whatever I find. I don't care if that person turns out to be some mental defective or prostitute. All these possibilities were in my mind, because they were possibilities. I said, "I will accept whatever I find and I will not cry about it. I will not add to my self pity."

I found out that my natural mother had two other sons. Both of them had committed suicide.

But to begin a search for one's birth mother is more than an act of curiosity; it is a step into the unknown that can lead to bitter disappointment or feelings of far greater complexity than simple joy. It is a time for caution, both of expectation and expression.

Candice Brown's motivation to search arose from strong emotions.

Why I've decided to search for my birth parents is that I want to know more about my background and why they did such an awful thing. It hurts me to know she got pregnant with me and they decided to give me up.

If I ever met my birth parents, first I would let them explain, then I would tell them to get out of my life. I will never forgive them for what they did to me. Never in a million years do I want to have a close relationship with them.

Sharon Russell was given up by birth parents who were happily married and had another child, and was never legally adopted. One of the reasons for her search is to find the answers to a puzzling question:

Finally, in my thirties, my stepfather gave me a few letters written to him by my birth father. It was very clearly stated that when they gave me up they only had enough time to spend with their young son and they felt they should make up for time lost. Strange. In reading the letters one gets the feeling that he was a well-educated, perhaps older, man. I also got the feeling that another child was possible for them in the future. He said they did not wish ever to have contact with me.

I was born in 1948, and I understand things may have been hard, but I haven't heard of people giving their children away at random, so to speak, because they didn't have enough time. If I ever meet my birth parents I would ask them to please give me a better reason for giving me away than that they didn't have enough time. That's the biggest hurt of all, and it doesn't seem to heal.

Needless to say, I am a strong supporter of abortion.

After struggling through an abused childhood, Marie Gee finally pulled her life together. Now that she has children of her own, she understands the terrible pain a mother goes through when she gives up a child. She continues to hope that she can uncover her true identity:

I find myself constantly looking at other people when we're out shopping or walking around and wondering if I'm looking at one of my real parents. All the while my soul is silently screaming, Where are you? Who are you? Are you still alive? Do you ever wonder about me and silently cry, too? Or was I just something that happened — wrong time, wrong place — and you would rather forget that I even exist? Either way, knowing something — good or bad as it may be — is still better than knowing nothing at all.

I suppose one of the reasons I've been searching for my real parents has been because of the lack of love from my adoptive parents, even to this day. I've always been treated as if I was someone else's child from as far back as I can remember. I think what hurts me the most now is the lack of love and attention from my adoptive parents towards their only two grandchildren. My children deserve more than I had as a child — so I had hoped, anyway.

Joe Soll did not even contemplate a search until his therapist suggested it in 1982. He had very negative feelings about his birth mother:

My shrink said, "You know, you can search for your birth mother."

I said, "Why would I want to search for that bitch?" I had proof that she didn't want me because she hadn't died.

She said, "You mean you can't think of any circumstances in which it might be okay for her to give you up?"

I became very vulgar and said, "No fucking way. There's no excuse, absolutely no excuse."

She pushed me to go to a support-group meeting. It took her nine months to get me to go. I said I wouldn't go because "there are going to be other people like me there" — I still couldn't use the word — "and they'll know about me." I finally went and arrived early and waited across the street until I saw somebody nice-looking. It happened to be the first person who walked in, who just looked earth mothery enough. I followed her up the stairs, and when we got to the top she turned around and said, "Are you here for the meeting?"

I said yes, and she asked, "Are you an adoptee?" She scared the shit out of me. I'd never even heard the word before. She said, "Welcome," and gave me a hug. I didn't even know "birth mothers" existed; I didn't know they'd be at the meeting. Most of my life I'd figured I was the only adopted kid in the world, except for Jamie McArthur, Helen Hayes's son. I figured that if there were only two adoptees there couldn't be a lot of birth mothers and they couldn't be human beings anyway. I listened to this woman's story and just started to cry. I was so moved, it flip-flopped my life. I walked out of the meeting three hours later wanting desperately to find my birth mother and saying the word "adoption." It was the three-hour transition of my life.

Patricia Sanders, an adoptee, is chair of the national conference for the American Adoption Congress and has been involved in the search movement for almost twenty years. She knew the names of both of her birth parents from a very early age:

I was very nosy; I just asked a lot of questions. My dad's cousin had been the social worker doing the placement, so they had a lot more information than most people do.

I think searching is something some people always do. You do it in the mind before you do it physically, and I didn't realize how much I used to fixate on searching until a few years ago. I ran into my best friend from high school. I said I was doing adoption searches. She said, "Don't you remember you used to sleep over and you would keep me awake all night saying, 'I need to search but I can't hurt my parents. How can I do it?'" I don't remember that. Obviously from a very early age I had a need to find out who I used to be and where I came from.

There's the "good" adoptee and the "bad" adoptee. In nearly every family with more than one adopted child you have the good adoptee who never wanted to rock the boat, never wanted to be cast out again — "You've taken me in. Does that mean you can get rid of me?" The other type of adoptee — me — probably at a very early age decided that I'd just see how bad I could be and what I could get away with. "Are they really going to try to send me back?" In many adoptive families, especially where you have a boy and girl, you will find this dichotomy between the good and bad adoptee.

The odd thing is that more women than men set out to search for their birth parents. I think it's societal. Men are not supposed to be weak; they're supposed to be self-sufficient. Looking for your mother isn't a manly thing to do. Men don't show emotion; they're not supposed to care. They're supposed to be self-made individuals — "I am who I am. Take me or leave me." Women are much more inclined to say, "I wish I knew."

Also women, especially as they get into their twenties and thirties and start having children, can relate very clearly to what it might be like to carry a child for nine months and then be parted from it. I think they can relate to the birth mother's child more than the men.

Even though you think about searching for many years, it's very typical for a woman to wait until you're married and have children and have a little time to think about who you are, not just being student, wife, mother, daughter. Especially after you have two or three children, as I did, and they don't look like you, and you think, "Maybe they don't look like me because I don't look like anyone." You need to know what you're passing on to them — medically, in talents and weaknesses — and you don't know.

It's only the white, Anglo cultures that seem to close up adoption, especially America and Canada. It's not done in the best interests of the child anymore. It's just like all the surrogacy and *in vitro* fertilization, to create a product for people who have a second car and a yacht; their lives are in order and all they're missing is a child. I get really upset about it because you don't create a human being as a product or commodity to be brokered.

For many adoptees, the idea of searching while their adoptive parents are still alive is unthinkable. Many fear hurting the people who have cared for them all their lives, and indeed some adoptive parents feel threatened if their children decide to search for their birth families. Susan Lumsden, however, was one of the lucky ones:

My adoptive parents were great. I received much love and support in all my growing years. I also had an adoptive brother to whom I am not close at all. I thought about searching for my birth mother many times as I was growing up, but I always decided against it because I didn't want to hurt my parents in any way. It was not that they wouldn't be behind me, because several times they told me that they would help in any way they could. However, I could sense that it would hurt them terribly if I did search for my birth mother. It wasn't until February 1991, after having lost both my parents to tragic illnesses, that I decided it was time to search.

Glynis Hill is another who decided to search for her birth mother after both her adoptive parents died:

This is something I had often thought about, particularly as I became older. Since having children of my own, the need to find my roots became very important to me.

Although at thirty-five I was happily married with three young daughters, I felt so alone. I was an only child, and although I was in contact with my adoptive father's family, after his death I felt that the last link with my birth had gone, together with the answers to so many questions.

After the initial shock of his death, I couldn't think of anything else but my birth family, and it became an obsession. I kept a lot of my feelings to myself, but my head was always buzzing. I held conversations and wrote letters in my head and even imagined situations (such as my being involved in an accident) that would force my family to be there for me. Every day I would wake up and it would all start again. Not a day would go by when I would not think of finding them.

Gloria Evans did not discover she was adopted until she was sixteen and stumbled across some papers in a trunk in her home in Newfoundland. She felt so thoroughly loved, however, that she felt no urge to search. It didn't occur to her to do so until tragedy struck years later:

In 1982 my adoptive mother became very ill with cancer, and it marked a turning point in my happy life. As I had no other siblings, I shouldered the whole responsibility for a person who had become more important to me than my own life. My mother came home from the hospital after having major surgery and had no bowel control. At that time our home had no toilet or water supply. We didn't have much in the way of luxuries, not even decent canvas on our floors. Sometimes we were cold, but it was the happiest time of my life. I was home and with the person I loved most in the world.

She suffered for close to five years. I had put myself and my children's needs on hold to care for her the only way I had been taught, that was with great love. In 1985, on a terribly cold Christmas Day, she died knowing that I loved her more than I will ever love another human being.

Since then I have had what people would describe as a very bad time. I will never be able to do without her and be happy and satisfied with my life. She gave me something that was so special, and I only wish I could be half the person she was.

Because of my inability to cope with losing her, I became very sick, physically and psychologically. Because of these illnesses I contacted the Post Adoption Department of Social Services to find out information on my birth family.

It was out of a sense of loyalty to her adoptive parents that Angela Netley postponed the search for her birth mother:

First, my dear but elderly adoptive father died. I started searching then but gave up. Then later, married with two little girls, I resumed my search, hoping to find a "Granny" for my children, thinking that perhaps my birth mother might be unmarried or might not have had any further children. My adoptive mother was a very cold person who failed to provide the love and understanding I needed, along with her stepson and her own son. The three of us to this day have had a very unsatisfactory relationship with her, as have our children, her grandchildren.

I hoped that by finding my own mother I'd find love from her and love for my children. After all, as a grown-up person in my thirties, I felt that I wouldn't be expecting too much from her and, if she had another family, then they'd be mature enough to understand my wish to find and identify with her.

Although he had lived in three foster homes by the time he was one year old, Jerry Appleton's life could not have been happier. In the third home he found all the love that any child could wish for. When he was an adult his adoptive mother became ill, and he naturally wanted to be with her:

I had enormous love for her — I ran to her side and stayed for as long as I could. In her last struggle — she died of cancer — she was transferred to Ottawa, to the cancer wing of the Civic Hospital. I just moved into the hotel next door and stayed. I would sit by her bedside and do whatever you can do in those horrible moments. You feel so helpless. She was a very giving, loving person. There wasn't enough she could do for people in her community. Over the years I can't tell you how many foster kids came through our house. Some of them kept in touch with her until her death, they were so attached to her.

There she was, lying in her bed, and I sat with her from morning till night, quietly reading while she was sleeping. One day she stirred and called out my name. I sat on the bed beside her and she said, "Jerry, I want you to promise me one thing."

Of course, I was so eager to please her and make her smile, I said, "Yes, name it and it's yours."

She said, "I want you to promise me that you will be happy."

Even though we have never ever spoken about adoption, from the time she told me when I was six until this moment when she was dying, I knew her heart understood my heart. I always knew that, but I felt I couldn't speak to her about it because I was afraid to hurt her. But there she was on her bed, making me promise that I would be happy, knowing full well what she was saying.

I joked and said, "Yes, yes."

She said, "No, I want you to say it in words to me."

I tried to laugh it off again, and she wouldn't let me. Finally she took my hand and said, "I want you to say it."

So I did. I said, "I promise I will be happy."

She smiled, closed her eyes and died.

The next week, after the funeral, my sister and I had to go into her apartment, which is a horrible thing to have to do. We had to find a paper of some sort. We went to the top drawer of her dresser, and it was almost empty. People who are dying play this wonderful game. They protect you by not speaking about it, and you protect them by not speaking about it. She knew; she had put all her house in order. In this top drawer there were two envelopes, white, a little yellowed by age. In her handwriting on one was my sister's name, Barbara, and on the other, my name.

We were a little surprised. I opened mine and found that what this dear, loving person had done — one last time she gave — was, in her last year, collected all the adoption information she had at her disposal and put it in two envelopes, one for Barbara and one for me. We stood there and cried.

Barbara had never searched, so everything she found was brand new to her. Everything in my envelope I had discovered by then. But the important thing was that it was my mother's permission to search. That was important to me. I had never spoken about it during my twenty-one-year search for fear of hurting her, even the slightest. This was her permission, and it meant everything to me.

Perhaps as hard as the decision to embark on the search for one's origins is the decision not to do so. Some adoptees feel less free to seek; others feel secure and do not need to complete the jigsaw. Joan Marshall, a counsellor and adoptee living in Ottawa, recognizes the difficult issues one must face in deciding to embark upon a search:

Anywhere you find a group of adoptees you will also find a lot of what I call "wallowing." These people don't want to resolve the issues; the biggest and most stable thing they have in their lives is not sorting out the issue of their adoption. Many of them don't want to give that up, so they repeat their stories over and over again, but never resolve them and don't move forward. When you are reunited with your birth parent you can't wallow anymore. You can't use it as a crutch; it's a very scary thing for many people.

My brother is also adopted and not related to me genetically at all. He's a very "good" adoptee. He said he couldn't do his search because he couldn't find his birth name, so I found it for him. The next thing was, "How do I contact these people? There are so many in Canada." So I found a hundred and sixty people in Canada with that last name, gave him the genealogy letter to write and told him to send them to those people. He never did it. Then he said, "Mom and Dad wouldn't want me to do that." But the world didn't fall apart for them because I did it. Then, "Oh, my wife wouldn't want me to do that," but when I asked her she said she had never said that. Then he said, "Well, it would disrupt the children." I haven't asked him anymore, but it might be the dog or the cat next time. Some adoptees build walls around themselves so they cannot find their birth parents. Silly me solved every one of his blocks, but he wants to be a Marshall. It's very important for him to be connected with his adoptive family. The unknown may not be as flowery and as filled with maids and chauffeurs as the adoptive story is. He may not want to give that up. I was ready to give it up and find the truth.

Susan Bell has learned a small amount about her birth parents, and this information, coupled with her beliefs on adoption, have led her to the decision not to search for them:

My feelings are very strong on whether you should search for your birth parents. They made the decision, however hard, to give you up for adoption. That should mean for life. If they only wanted a short period of time, fostering should have been thought of.

My parents adopted me because they were unable to have their own children and were, therefore, wanting to provide love and opportunity, to make their lives complete and also mine. To find their daughter looking for her original parents would, I feel, cause hurt and damage to all concerned. Life is too short to cause such pain.

To those thinking of looking for their real parents, I would say don't! Be happy with what you've got. Someone wanted you; don't make them feel unwanted.

Although Rick Magill had known he was adopted from the time he was twelve and says that it did cause him "periods of self-doubt and other anxieties," he too has little inclination to solve the mystery of his past:

I admit to wanting to know my biological family's medical history, both for myself and out of concern for my child, but beyond this I don't have even the slightest desire to obtain further information or to establish contact. Nor do I understand the need of others to do so.

I was raised by a loving mother and father who were, and still are, there for me when I needed help and guidance. My birth parents, on the other hand, for whatever reason, were not able to do so. I hold no animosity or feelings of rejection over this, as adoption is a mere fact of life and has been for all of history. I truly cannot understand the need that many adoptees have to contact individuals who have no more input into or impact on their lives than any other unknown person in the world. Will test-tube babies search for their birth parents? The value that it supposedly adds to their lives escapes me, but at the same time the pain it must cause the adoptive parents to see this need in their children is obvious.

At the risk of being cruel or unsympathetic, I must say that it seems to me that these adoptees must have been raised in homes where they were not given the degree of love and attention that a child needs and that they therefore feel that something is lacking in their lives. If I were to meet my birth parents, about all I would want to say is a thank you for giving me the opportunity to grow up with the real parents I have had.

Abbigale Patterson was able to trace her birth mother through the Department of Social Services in Halifax. What she found was not what she had hoped for, however, and confronted with this information, Abbigale decided to give up her search:

The real shock came in the last paragraph when the Department of Social Services said that, yes, I did have brothers and a sister. My mother had had three children before I came along, and she had given them all up for adoption. I was finally disgusted by her cavorting all over the province, becoming pregnant (For heaven's sake, I thought, why didn't she use birth control?) and leaving children all over the place to be adopted and wonder for the rest of their lives who she is. I was angry at her all over again.

More quickly this time, my father's words came back to me. Okay, I thought, at least she didn't abort me. I was given up to a great set of parents, and she did do the right thing by allowing me to be adopted rather than keeping me and trying to raise me herself. What a scary prospect that might have been.

The search has ended, probably forever. I have no wish to meet her now. I still wonder from time to time if she is alive now, if she thinks about the children she has given up. If maybe she finally did marry. I hope so. I am her daughter, after all, and I would hope that she finally found someone to share her life with and have her own family. I think about who I look like and when someone says, "You know, you look a lot like a friend of mine," I get uneasy, thinking that this person could actually be my brother or sister, or a niece or nephew. I do believe my natural mother made the right choice in not aborting me and allowing me to be adopted. She did give me a better life than, I'm sure, she could have provided.

I do wish her happiness and thank her for her choice!

Brian Blain admits he has not given the idea of a search too much thought and is avoiding taking action until he feels he has more accomplishments under his belt:

One underlying thought was whether or not I was worthy. Would I be a pleasant surprise? I can answer my own doubts better than anyone, I suppose, because I also had a daughter when I was sixteen, and she was given up for adoption. Would I reject her if she arrived on my doorstep without having attained material success? Of course not. I'm sure I would accept and even love her unconditionally. So I suppose I could assume that same kind of acceptance if I should meet my birth parents.

Marilyn Fefchak was the product of her mother's affair outside marriage. She is very understanding that her mother's husband did not wish to raise her:

My birth father had no way of raising me at that point, but he visited the foster home shortly before my adoption and gave me a teddy bear.

I have never wished to make contact. I have only pleasant thoughts of the two people who made sure I would be given a better chance in life. I'm thankful for the life I was given. My roots are here in this place with these people who have been my family as long as I can remember. So instead of root-searching, I spend time helping those ageing folks who gave completely to me for all those years.

The feelings surface when someone says, "You look like

someone I've seen." I'm sure I do. I carry a lot of someone's personality, sense of humour and many other inherited traits, including a quick temper. Oh, yes, the thoughts of the people who made my life possible often surface, but the need to find my roots before I can find myself has never been an issue. But I still have that teddy bear that young father gave me so many years ago.

6

My Child Is Out There Somewhere

I may never know you, or know about you, but until I draw my last breath I will never forget you, have never forgotten you.

Myra London

THROUGHOUT HER LIFE, *the mother who has given up a child for adoption may suffer the agony of never knowing where her child is. Birthdays, Christmas, children at play, all may bring the fateful day to the surface and with it the unanswered questions: Where is she? Is she well? Does she know of my existence? Will I ever see her again? And worst of all: Does she hate me for what I did? Some mothers harbour fierce resentment at the lack of information and choice available to them at the time of adoption, and are distressed and angry that so little help is offered in tracing their child. (A birth parent has no right to information about her offspring; she can only register for a match and hope she will be contacted.) Others express no such regrets but are often equally haunted by thoughts of their lost child. There is much evidence of suppressed emotion and consequently physical and emotional illness.*

For years after she gave up her son for adoption, Rishy Powell
suffered both physically and emotionally from her guilt:

I told my future husband before we were married. He said it
didn't matter to him because what happened had happened
before he met me and he loved me and he wanted to marry me
and live happily ever after. Before I got married my aunt had told
me not to tell my husband, that if I did he'd throw it in my face
every time we had an argument. I had to tell him, and he never
threw it in my face. He supported me.

When I got pregnant with my husband's baby, I developed
horrendous pains, as if I was having a miscarriage. Khrone's
disease is brought about by a lot of stress and anxiety, and also
guilt. I felt a lot of guilt that I couldn't account for; I didn't know
where it was coming from. Then when I had my second son, for
eight months I had spastic bowel attacks.

After I gave birth to this son, I was very depressed. I couldn't
understand it. I loved kids; I was the best babysitter on the block.
I had so much love to give, but I was so depressed. The doctor
said that if I didn't snap out of it, he would have to put me away.
I snapped out of it fast. I would get horrendous pains in my
stomach, like labour pains, for a year. They would be ten hours
in coming and would stay for ten hours. I never had any relief
for a year. That was guilt. You know when I got rid of it? I
blamed my mother all these years for giving up my baby, and I
never realized it. It was like I was choking on something; it was
so bad that I had to talk to someone. My husband was my
psychiatrist, but I just couldn't get it out. Finally I got it out and
said, "I think I hate my mother." After I said that I never had a
spastic bowel attack again! So, I really blamed my mother for
giving up my son.

Finally that passed, and then I got pregnant again. It wasn't
so bad while I was pregnant, but afterwards the same thing
happened for six months — these horrible pains. But when I had

my next child it was the most beautiful thing in the world — I had no pain, no depression. He was such a delight, so wonderful. I can't describe it; it was so different. Maybe because it was five years later; maybe I was in a different frame of mind, I don't know.

I would automatically think of my first child on each of his birthdays. When my kids were growing up, and we were having a lot of drug problems with the two older ones, I always used to wonder if the son I gave away was having all these problems. Was he having problems because I gave him away? I brought the blame on myself again. Was he looking for me? Who did he look like? What was he doing? Was he getting into trouble? Was he happy? What if he were to appear on my doorstep? When I saw kids who were blue-eyed with blond hair, I'd think they could maybe be him.

Mary-Jane Brodie was on her first long trip away from her St. Thomas, Ontario, home when memories stopped her in her tracks:

I woke up in a cozy little motel room in Tucson, Arizona. Oh, it was great to be alive! I flipped on the radio to hear the day's weather report, and the first words the newscaster spoke were "It's March 24th." My whole world stopped. It was the eighteenth birthday of my daughter Connie, the child I had given up for adoption in 1969. Not that I ever forgot — not once in the past eighteen years — but this birthday suddenly crept up on me. It must have been because of the excitement of the trip. Frank, my wonderful husband, cradled me in his arms as he had done many, many times before, while I cried and wailed about the daughter I had given up for adoption. Apparently the cord severed at birth wasn't the one attached to this mother's heart.

If only I had known that day that I would personally hand her her nineteenth birthday present the next year!

Judith Kizell-Brans, a birth mother, adoptee and counsellor in adoption issues, makes the point that the pain of a birth mother's loss can recur years later in another guise:

If you are unable to resolve a loss at the time, it reappears at a time when another loss presents itself. Many of us in adoption have so successfully buried our true feelings that getting in touch with ourselves takes years. Many of us do not recognize fully the impact that surrendering a child had on our lives, relationships and careers. It makes experiencing other normal life losses, such as changing homes, jobs, relationships, more painful for us.

Brenda Hobbs has suffered from depression and feelings of worthlessness since she gave her daughter, Dawn, up for adoption. Her anguish seems to stem from society's expectation that she should forget her experience and get on with her life:

I have been living with loss and grief for seventeen years when my mother died, four days before my daughter's birthday. One year later I sought grief counselling, as I had been unable to stop crying, unable to accept my loss. It is not until now that I realize I was not only grieving for my mother but also for the loss of the child I had given up and not been encouraged to grieve for. In fact, the word "grief" was never associated with relinquishment — not with birth, only with death. I was expected to forget it and get on with my life, even though the greatest part of my life was missing.

For several years after her birth, even when we were no longer a couple, Bill and I would have dinner together, complete with birthday cake, to celebrate our child's birthday. But that isn't the only day I've thought of her all these years. She's never far from my mind. I have no other children. Dawn is my one and only.

At the time of relinquishment, I was told by my social worker that I was doing a good deed in giving a child to a family that wanted one but couldn't have one, and that I should be happy to provide this. Yes, this was perhaps a nice way to make me feel good about myself, but no one ever asked how I really felt — no one ever asked me about grief and loss.

Emotionally, I feel very underdeveloped. I have tremendous fear of commitment in relationships and have difficulty trusting people enough to develop friendships. I have always been reluctant to get involved with people, but when I do and the relationship breaks down, it takes me a very long time to get over it. Consequently, rather than get involved, I live on the outside, on the fringe, seldom committing, and when I do it is with others who have also experienced some form of loss.

Learning that I cannot carry another child may have been a relief for me, as I was always afraid of losing another baby, of feeling that same sense of deprivation. My conscious thoughts surrounding childbirth always focussed on pain, hence not wanting to have another child. I am starting to realize why for the past twenty-odd years I have been depressed more than not, off in a world of my own.

"Life goes on," friends of birth mothers tell them, but it can be almost impossible to live as though the relinquishment of a child could be forgotten, as Pat Tyler recalls:

Afterwards I got a job. I had to get out of the house and wanted to replace what I had lost, so I married the first man who came along. It was a bad choice; I wouldn't have married him had it not been for those very pressing emotional needs. So that was a short-lived situation. Then I lived on my own for many years. I worked hard at repressing my emotions, keeping my feelings about giving up my baby down, not allowing too many thoughts about it. Not that I wouldn't think about it, but I wouldn't allow myself to dwell on it because it would just tear me apart. When you're that traumatized, even if you have someone to talk to you probably can't talk to them anyway.

I see this experience as being very close to that of having your child abducted. Usually in those cases there's violence and possibly a death, so this isn't quite that bad. My mind can't even come to grips with how those mothers feel. But it's worse than a death, because in a death you can grieve and close the coffin. This is something like a family member being a prisoner of war. They might be alive, but you don't know that, and there's that loss as if they're dead. You can never really come to grips with that or accept it because there's no final death, you can't come to grips with touching a loved one who's dead.

All we were told is that our children were given good homes. I could give my son a mother, but I couldn't give him a father. That was important to me because I didn't have a father. Also it was the social situation of the day — single parenthood was rare. A "good home" to me was a two-parent family, churchgoers, good income, value placed on education — perfect people. But now, twenty-eight years later, I learned that adoption didn't always deliver perfection. What really hit me as a blow not too long after I placed my son for adoption was that my girlfriend's mother adopted a son. I thought, How could she? She was old, a divorcee who had remarried — she wasn't perfect. That was a shock. Then when I found out later that my son's situation was less than perfect I really felt cheated. If there had been some help for me, at least he would have had his mother. I really feel very short-changed about that.

Sometimes, over the years, when I'd been drinking, I would break down and cry. On those occasions I would sometimes, from time to time, reveal myself to friends and get into a state of feeling very sorry for myself, very inadequate and very condemned.

Even though I'd just turned twenty-one when he was born, I was treated like a child by my social worker. My legal rights were presented to me in this manner: "You will not be able to see your son again, nor will he be able to see you." I can remember saying to myself that some day he'd grow up and that she was wrong; I'd meet him some day. I knew it, even though in those days it was impossible. There was no registry, and I really didn't know about adoptees coming back and seeking information. I guess deep down I hoped he'd find me one day or I would find him.

But over the years you begin to believe it would be impossible to find your child. In the meantime two decades elapsed. Then I discovered Parent Finders and started reading books about the pain adoptees experience. I started digging and researching because none of this was ever told to me. I came across a paper my social worker had written in 1958, in which she talked about adoptees coming back to the Children's Aid Society and wanting information and wanting to make contact with their birth parents. She never told me that. All that was kept secret from me. You were stonewalled. In the paper she talked about the severe pain adoptees may experience. How does that make you feel, twenty years later, when you've suffered for all those years and now you find a paper describing all this? Maybe I would have tried to find a way to keep him. But you were also made aware that if you tried to keep your baby, eight months later they might come in and try to take it, then your baby would have little hope of getting a good home. There was too much at stake for the baby to make more than one mistake.

My attitude today is to ask, Why not find more mature adoptive parents who can accept the open concept of adoption, as in other cultures where children are placed in other families but can see their biological parents and that's accepted. Why can't a birth parent be like an aunt or uncle? It's the adoptive parents who want the secrecy. We didn't have the financial wherewithal to keep our children, so the government came in to take babies away from a poor group and give them to another group. Unfortunately, in the sixties there were too many babies, so there was a scramble to find homes for them, but there was no concept of trying to help us keep them. It wasn't until 1968 that single mothers could get welfare in Canada. People don't give up their children because they want to — it's financial.

I ended up visiting a psychiatrist for almost two years, but I wouldn't speak. I didn't know what was troubling me. I guess I thought I was supposed to forget about my son. I hardly said two words. I would sit for my hour in silence. Slowly he tried to get into my feelings about surrendering my child and tried to bring this out, but as soon as he did that I wouldn't go back. There was no way I could get those feelings out. I had to repress it again until I had my next boy, Steven, in 1978 and it rekindled all those feelings. I can remember changing his diaper when he was just an infant, with tears streaming down my cheeks, thinking that I didn't even change the diapers of my first baby.

Maria Lynch's youngest daughter was adopted at the age of three:

This was a direct result of my suffering from a mental illness, and at the time my husband and I felt it was the only option open to us. Other possibilities, such as long-term fostering, were not explained to us, and I am left with a great deal of resentment at the way in which things were handled by the social workers. It was a time of great distress for us, and our older children were affected by this adoption, too. Over the years the whole family thought of Fiona. Birthdays and Christmas were especially painful.

Myra London is one who does not regret her decision, but she says she often thinks about being able to write to her son, whom she has not seen since 1957. If she could send him a letter, this is part of what she would say:

After your birth I took you back to the home and cared for you for ten days before driving to the Children's Aid Society with my sister, where your adoptive parents waited.

Ten days! Even now I remember every movement you made, and you were beautiful. I don't regret my decision, as your birth father was also very young and our chances of giving you a good life at that time were impossible.

My feelings from my heart are not that I want to meet you or interfere after all these years, even though I am registered with the Children's Aid Society. To my knowledge you have never inquired after me.

All I really want to know, have a tremendous need to know, is if you had a good life. Did I do all the right things that were expected of me at that time? Was the decision I was pressured into the right one? I was told by the Children's Aid Society that it was a "good" adoption. What the hell does that mean? Believe me, all you get for your questions are stone-faced stares from the people who hold the knowledge.

I may never know you, or know about you, but until I draw my last breath I will never, and have never, forgotten you.

Margaret Rose expresses succinctly the feelings of most birth mothers who are forced to live their life without knowing the destiny of their child:

In 1968 I gave birth to an eight-pound baby boy. Later I gave him up for adoption. From that day on there is not one day I have not thought of him. I thought it was better for him — I hope it was.

His father already had a family. I didn't want to break that up. I thought of them at the time, not of myself.

I am still single and have no other children. I'd love to see him just once. Not to interfere, just to see he is well.

Laura Robinson in Moncton is another woman haunted by her lost child:

I never stopped thinking about her. What does she look like? What colour is her hair? Does she look like me? Is she healthy? Are her parents good to her? Will she ever want to find me? What will I say to her? Will she ever forgive me? These are some of the questions I ask every day.

When I think back, I've never regretted my decision, and each year that goes by I pray God will some day bring us back together. I still feel a great loss in my life, like a big hole that was never filled, as if there is something missing. I've thought of having other children, maybe trying to have another girl, hoping this would fill that spot, but I believe nothing will until I meet her.

Jean Clark feels much the same:

I knew what she looked like when she was born. I knew she was fair, and when I saw a tall slender girl, I would wonder if that was her. I wondered what she looked like, and I wondered if she was okay, I wondered if she was healthy, and I wondered and I wondered . . .

Not all birth parents decide to search for their sons and daughters, however. Having grown up in a troubled household in London, Ontario, Eleanor Willis knew she wanted more for her son. Much as she loves him, she decided not to search:

Today, Christopher Joseph, you celebrate your twenty-seventh birthday. You are almost as old as I was when I gave birth. I have never searched for you and probably never will. I gave you your first breath, and I am sure your family has given you all the things I wanted for you: love, understanding, a happy life, an education, an opportunity to develop your talents and skills and a sense of well-being. It doesn't matter where you are, I somehow can envisage you. I love you and I love your family. I hope one day our paths will cross, but that will have to be your choice and your decision.

If a single, pregnant woman were to ask me for advice on this subject today, I would say, "Do whatever you think is best for the child. No matter what decision you make, it will affect your emotions for the rest of your life." My decision was the right one for me at that time. To this day I have no regrets.

Arriving at the decision to search for one's child is seldom easy for a birth parent. Many more women than men decide to attempt contact, although some fathers do sign on to the various contact registers available. Others are unaware that they have even sired a child.

Women who do decide to initiate a search have many anxieties. How will the child feel about this mother who has suddenly appeared from the past? How will the adoptive family react to this intrusion? Does the condemnation she felt years ago still exist? If her baby was born out of wedlock she was seen as the villain at the time. But worse than that, she committed the unpardonable sin of giving her child to another — a child who may now sit in judgement.

There may also be problems with the birth parent's present family. When Judy Anne Brooks was debating whether or not to search for her son Shane and her daughter Shannon, she faced a threat to her marriage:

Every birthday, every Christmas and every day of the year I thought of Shane and Shannon, and I still do. I had another child and was so afraid of losing her, too.

I married Tom in 1983. He can't accept the fact that I have two other children. He was there with me in Edmonton and saw them, but he won't have anything to do with them. So I just kept quiet about them in front of him. I told only a few of my friends about my children. A lot of people just classify me as a terrible person for giving them up. They don't understand and never will unless it happens to them. There were times I wanted to find Shane and Shannon, so I contacted Edmonton welfare, and they told me they had been adopted into separate families. I was really upset that they separated them again.

By now I was getting really tired of having to keep quiet about it in front of Tom. I was getting to the point that I didn't care what Tom thought; those children were my flesh and blood. So I stopped hiding from Tom the fact that I was in touch with Parent Finders in Edmonton, and he was really angry. I was serious when I told him that Shane was now eighteen years old and he had every right to know now who his mother is and, if by chance, Shane happened to contact me and wanted to see me, he'd definitely be welcome in my world. If Tom couldn't accept that fact by then, then he could get out of my life forever. We've been together for thirteen years, and I'll throw it all away if I have to. I told him Shane is my son, and he's going to have to accept it whether he likes it or not. Tom told me Shane can come and stay, but only for one day when he's out. I just kept quiet because I know that I'll throw Tom out.

Since the law started about a child having the right to know his birth parents when he turns eighteen, I've been dreaming every day and wishing every day for Shane to hurry and be eighteen. I thought the day he turns eighteen he's going to call me, so I started fantasizing about that day. I thought, I am going to be so old. I hope I don't scare him away. I was going to be thirty-five years old, and I started a diet to look good for him. My spirits really started to perk up, but I still had that lost, empty feeling inside me and felt so alone, lost, guilty and worried. I was constantly wondering, Is that my child? Are they okay? Do they miss me like I miss them? Are they happy? Are they being abused? I pray to God, please let Shane and Shannon want to find me. Please don't let them be angry with me. I love them very much and am always thinking of them.

Shane has turned eighteen now, and it came before I knew it. I didn't lose weight, and I still look more or less the same, only greyer. Now I'm really sad because I'm so afraid Shane will never have the desire to find me, and that will just tear me apart.

Shane and Shannon, wherever you are, I love you and will always love you. Please come and see me. I want to explain to you what happened, to tell you it wasn't my fault. I wanted to keep you but I couldn't. Please understand. Please don't hate me. Come home to me so I can hold you in my arms again. This time I'll be sure to never, never let go again.

Despite her own terrible suffering, Mary Anne Cohen's counsellors had convinced her that her child would be happy in his adoptive home. Then she contacted the ALMA Reunion Registry in New York:

In 1975 I heard about ALMA and was shocked to hear that adoptees might want to know their original parents and even more shocked to hear that many adoptees felt abandoned and unloved. I had thought I would suffer but truly believed that I had done the right thing for my child and that all adoptees were perfectly happy. My rage knew no bounds, to hear this was not true and that I may have hurt my son as well as myself. I immediately began to search.

Although it is much less common for a birth father to search for his child, when he does he may be met with even less sympathy than the birth mother. Robin Wise lives with the pain of his still unfulfilled quest:

I couldn't talk to anyone about it, I couldn't do anything; I had no rights. I moved to Canada in 1970 and hadn't told anyone. I told my wife, and she's only mentioned it once in anger, so I can't even talk about it with her. I have children, but they don't know.

I carried it around for years and years and wanted to do something about it, and I couldn't. Every time I talked to civil servants I hit a blank wall. It was devastating. Most men would have said, "I was lucky; I didn't have to pay maintenance or anything." But I would have far rather paid that.

An additional difficulty for men may be in tracing the child's mother. Robin had immigrated to Canada, but went back to England to search first for the mother of his child and, through her, for his son:

I didn't know where to go, where to start, what to do. Everything was a brick wall. Her family hid her, buried her. I went to her sister and said I'd really like to talk to her and would she please ask her. For three years she wouldn't ask her. I begged and pleaded and said I just wanted to talk to her.

Then I realized I could go to St. Catherine's House and search through the records, which I did. I had no idea where she lived, what her married name was, nothing. I went into the Green Room at St. Catherine's House, with the marriage indexes, and searched for the date she got married. Then, when I found out what her married name was, the next trick was to find out where she lived.

It was Christmas 1970, and I went to her parents and said, "I want to know what's going on." They didn't like seeing me again, but they didn't have any choice. They couldn't have cared less about her. I asked where she was. They wouldn't tell me but did let slip that she was in a certain area.

A year ago I went to the library. Her name wasn't that common. I looked and looked and looked until I found what I was searching for. I had to go through numerous phone books, but I remembered where her mother said she was.

When I started to talk about searching about ten years ago, my mother thought it would be better if I didn't disturb any hornets' nests. I've never said anything to her about it since. My dad knows. He says, "Nobody realized what this did to you." He's been very good. The last time I was in England, he knew I was going to the library; I came back grinning because I'd found her name. I needed to find out if it was really her, and he said we could find out from the list of voters. So we had to cook up a story about why we were going for a drive. The town where she lives is one of my mother's favourites, so we couldn't tell her where we were going or she'd want to come with us. We asked for the list of voters, and lo and behold it was her.

I don't want to go to her; I don't want anything to do with her. I don't know how she feels. I can't hang too much hope on finding my son. I'll try because I'll have to. In case it never happens I can't hang my heart on it. I am now on the NORCAP register.

I think about my son all the time, but it's something you have to keep under control.

Valerie Hamilton was able to be optimistic. She confesses to being a naturally curious person and was convinced that the daughter she had given up for adoption would have inherited the same curiosity:

If she was anything like me I knew she'd be wanting to find out about her heritage, and that's how it turned out. The day after her eighteenth birthday she went to a British registry office. It took a few months, and when they finally advised me that she had been there — in retrospect it was amusing — it was in a letter saying, "We have something that may be of interest to you. . . ."

7

I Just Want to Tell Her
I Forgive Her

*Here I am, almost face to face with
what I have been searching for for so
long. I'm not sure how to feel —
excited, scared, cautious.*

Rachel Derry

D ESPITE THE ASSISTANCE *now available to adoptees, they
have no guarantee of ever tracking down their birth
parents. Bureaucratic red tape and nagging doubts can
delay and discourage. Is this emotional rollercoaster worth the
risk? Will the truth be worse than not knowing? Will the adoptee
be considered an intruder rather than a dream come true?*

*Jane Reeves was twenty-five and had thought about searching
for many years when she decided to stop procrastinating and
look for her birth family. Why had she not tried before?*

I was basically very scared. I had felt a sense of rejection, not, I
hasten to add, from my adoptive parents but from the woman
who had given her baby away.

I wrote to Somerset House only to receive a copy of the same
birth certificate I already had, the adopted one. I was told that
the other certificate could not be released without counselling.

Daft, I first thought, but later I realized how sensible this probably was.

After some wait an appointment was made, and I learned a little about my early life. I was shocked. When I was born my mother was twenty-five, a lot older than I expected. I had been given up for adoption when I was six weeks old, and she had breastfed me until I was handed over. This seemed very odd to me, but I was told she had no home to take me to and was almost pressured to give me up for adoption.

I was then asked why I wanted to see her. At this stage I wasn't sure that I actually did want to see her. I was still hurting, really. However, I felt she had a right to know what had happened to her daughter. I have always believed that any mother must always wonder about her child. I felt she needed to know that what she did was right. I really couldn't have wished for a better home to be brought up in.

It took the adoption agency at least six weeks to find my birth mother, which seemed an eternity once I had made the first steps. However, when I finally got the news that they had found her and that she was overjoyed, I was quite shocked. What to say and how to treat her? I really had no idea. The adoption agency in St. Albans was great, a Church of England group, but I don't think they really fully understood. I don't think anyone, unless they are in the same situation, can.

Rachel Derry's birth parents had been married when she was born, although they were very young and living as hippies in a commune. She had been told that her father could not adjust to life with a crying baby and had left. Consequently, when Rachel decided to embark upon her search she wished only to locate her birth mother, having a natural resentment towards her father.

In December I got a phone call saying that my natural mother couldn't be found, but they had found my father. Did I want to meet him? So many emotions ran through me. I had been very, very angry with him. I knew so little about him, and what I did know I didn't like. But I decided to say yes because, well, I was afraid that I wouldn't have another chance and maybe he could lead me to my mother.

It is so hard to communicate the feelings involved in this type of situation. I have struggled all my life to explain to people what it feels like. I grew up in a wonderful home with two parents who love me and a supportive sister and brother. I was extremely lucky. Yet it's like a hole inside. I was/am not whole. My history is borrowed. My adoptive parents stem from England and Ireland. But it has never been my history, my ancestry — there is a big difference — and a voice in my head would always say, Well, that's not you. I think this is one of the most important things for me to learn. Why do I have dark hair? Am I Irish? Jewish? Do I come from a line of gypsies? Royalty?

In essence I think I want to know that I belong. I'm not just a blip on this earth. I have a past that is in my blood, my hair, my skin, and I'm continuing that line. For example, when my natural father contacted the social worker, he gave tidbits of information about the family history. I found out that I have great-great relatives who were vaudeville performers — and here I am an actor!

But the most astounding news was that my grandfather was Jewish. I now share a history! I can point and say I belong to your past. It's inside me, even though I was raised in the Protestant faith. So I am eagerly awaiting news about where I'm from, what country. What language did my ancestors speak? Little things, seemingly insignificant but not. The next thing I think is important for us to share is a sense of physical similarity. Do I actually look like another person? Whose nose do I have? Did he/she bite his/her nails like I do?

It also fills me with fear. I have had this uniqueness of being adopted about me for so long, and I'm slowly losing it. Here I am, almost face-to-face with what I have been searching for for so long. I'm not sure how to feel — excited, scared, cautious? All of these things bubble inside and sometimes it's hard to pinpoint the main emotion.

The search for one's past can be long and frustrating, sometimes taking many years. Jerry Appleton found his birth mother after only six months of concentrated searching, though he had been travelling that journey in his mind for much longer.

Over twenty-one years I had found little pieces of information, and slowly a picture formed. I had played a game in my head. Whenever I was in a town in eastern Ontario, I would look in the phone book under the name Martin, my birth mother's maiden name. I would count them; I would read their first names; I would look at their addresses. As the years progressed, I started calling them, trying to find her. Her name was Evangeline; Eve they called her. I got very good at it. The deception was clever, and that's what the process taught you to do — to be deceitful for your own positive end. I would pretend that I was the assistant to the deputy minister of census measurement. You'd be surprised how much information people will volunteer! Or, equally, I would simply say on the phone that I was a driver for Simpson Sears and that I had a parcel for this lady, and could they help me. People are so generous, and they would help. I found nothing. That game lasted probably eight or nine years.

After my adoptive mother died and gave me that permission to search, I was reluctant. I felt as if I was deceiving my mother, as if I was betraying her. A few months later I came to peace with that and resumed the search.

I found myself in Cornwall, Ontario. This time I did it differently. I went to the research library in the town and went through the microfiche, back to 1938 to 1942, and found people who were of my birth mother's age. Then, through the city directories, I found twenty-one Martins about her age, male and female. None of them was called Evangeline. I was thinking that, in this twenty-one there had to be a cousin or brother, a nephew or niece.

Then I followed them, book by book by book, from the '40s to the year 1990. By the time I got there, ten of the twenty-one were still in Cornwall. The other eleven had either died or moved away. So I went back to my motel room, sat down and called each of the ten. Quickly I got, "No, I don't know her." One sweet, kind lady said, "Yes, I knew her. She died about ten years ago." I was hearing about my mother's death. We talked a little more, and I thought I'd try to find out more about the family. Then we realized we were talking about two different people. It was not my mother. I can't tell you the joy in my heart.

Every time I dialled the tenth number there was no answer, and I did this all day on the Saturday. I got up the next morning, dialled — no answer. I had to come back to Toronto, so at one point I decided I must leave. I packed, checked out, and I don't know why, but something made me fib to the lady behind the desk. I told her I had forgotten something in the room. I went back, dialled and a man answered. His name was Alphonse Martin, as French as you could find, but he spoke English like the king of England.

We chatted. He was an absolutely pleasant gentleman. I lied to him and said my mother had given me the name Evangeline Martin and told me to call her and say hello — she was an old friend — and that I couldn't find her name in the phone book, and could he help me? There was a pause, he giggled and said, "The most beautiful woman in the world."

I said, "How do you mean?"

He said, "Inside and outside. She's my sister." I was talking to my uncle.

I said, "Do you mind if I ask some questions about the family?"

He said, "No, I love this. I'm retired and my hobby is genealogy."
I looked up to the skies and said thank you.

We talked for about forty minutes. I couldn't tell him who I was because I had no knowledge of whether my birth mother had shared this with anyone. As it turned out, he didn't know, so my caution was well placed. He gave me her phone number and address. He said she was well and had been married for some forty years to the most wonderful human being on earth. They had no children, but they loved life and had been around the world three or four times. It was wonderful to hear that much positive information about my mother because I had worried about her.

He said, "I want you to come over. We'll have a glass of wine and talk more." I wanted so badly to do that, but I turned down his invitation because I didn't want to go into his home and lie, with the thought that somewhere along the line I might have to confront him and say I'd lied.

I came back to Toronto, and for the first time in my life, I knew where my mother lived: I could write to her. I knew her number: I could call her.

As a teenager, Christopher Berriman had experienced periods of obsession over the circumstances of his adoption. Nevertheless, it was not until he was in his late twenties that he began his search:

Suddenly I thought that even if my mother wanted to contact me she couldn't because of the legalities surrounding adoption. I decided to start my search and went to see a social services counsellor, as I was required to do by law. He was very helpful in advising how I should go about my search. I had read how long and frustrating a search can be, but I was fortunate that everything fell into place very easily. Less than three months later I had found my birth mother.

I was ecstatic and frightened at the same time. We exchanged letters and photographs to familiarize ourselves with each other. I was absolutely overwhelmed to discover that I had a brother and a sister and that they were excited about meeting me.

My mother put her telephone number on her second letter. It took me four days to pluck up the courage to ring. I kept dialling and putting the phone down. Eventually I let it ring until she answered it. She was very nervous and emotional, as was I. My heart was beating so fast I thought it was going to explode. We arranged that my wife and I would meet her in a hotel near where she lived.

Growing up in a French-Canadian home in Toronto, André Chamberlain remembers fantasizing about the identities of his birth parents. His search and reunion led to a surprise about his origins:

When I was twenty-eight, in October 1990, I felt it was time. I called the Centre de Services Sociaux, and they sent me an application form. I filled it in, and by the end of November I received all nonidentifying information regarding my adoption. They noted that my request to meet my birth mother would be followed up by one of their workers in the near future.

In a P.S. at the bottom of the letter, they also mentioned that, since my mother was native Canadian, I might consider applying for status under the Indian Act. In fact, from the nonidentifying information I found out that both my parents were native.

My adoptive parents had never been told. I don't seem to have a stereotypical native appearance. Luckily I have worked with the native community in the field of mental health and, having made a few friends, have developed a great deal of respect for the community. The thought has crossed my mind, What if I had been a redneck?

In deciding to search for birth parents, adoptees are probably taking the first decision they have been allowed to make regarding their own adoption and origins. Gloria Evans describes it as moving out of a situation of limbo. After caring for her dying adoptive mother through a long illness, she decided to try to find her birth family:

I've come to learn that there are no silver linings and there's certainly no gold at the end of the rainbow, no young mother waiting to hear if the baby she gave up was properly taken care of. The information I got hurt me.

My profile told me that my birth mother had me when she was thirty-three years old, that she was of very low intelligence, couldn't learn and had no education. She had had brain surgery the year before I was born. I also found out I had a brother and sister at the time of my birth. My mother had never married and was taken care of, along with the two children, by her mother. I don't know where they live or anything more about them, just my surname.

My worker at the Post Adoption Department understands my hurt and my desperation to find a connection with my brother and sister. There's almost a kind of urgency on my part. I've loved and been loved all my life, but there's an emptiness that my adoptive mother left that can never be filled. Sometimes I hold onto my life by a very fine thread, hoping and wishing I could have her back, knowing I never can.

If I met my birth mother I couldn't be bitter. I'd have to let her know that I thank her for giving me the life I had with my mother. I wouldn't have had the chance to know that kind of dedication and love if she hadn't given me up.

After his adoptive father died and he was sorting through his papers, Robert Kool found material relating to his adoption. It was enough to prompt him to seek out his birth mother. The search led him to a small Maritime village shop, where he co-opted the assistant behind the counter:

I'm standing there in this little shop, and this little old lady is on the phone, probably to my grandmother. She passes the phone to me to talk to her. I'm invited up and given directions. A tall lady with snow-white hair greets me at the door. We sit at the kitchen table with her little husband. She's across from me, he's at the end of the table, to my right. She says, "I know who you are. Do you know who you are?"

I said, "I know who I am. Do you know who you are?" Neither one of us would say it.

She said, "You're my grandson. Can I phone your mother?" She got up and hugged me. She was crying.

She said on the phone, "I have a grandson here . . . not Todd . . . it's, yes . . . he's found you."

When Paul Patterson decided to search for his birth mother it was not on a sudden impulse. He had thought it over carefully:

I always knew some day that I would search, but I wanted to wait until I was mature enough to be able to do it. If I was to search out my birth parents and find total rejection again — that would be rejection twice — that would be hard to deal with. I wanted to be mature enough to handle that properly.

I went down to the Children's Aid Society and said, "Here I am, this is what I want to do. Let's get it happening." The social worker and I filled out all the paperwork; then I had to go to the Adoption Disclosure Registry, and they set up the paperwork there. Then they told me it could be a seven-year wait, so I wasn't too thrilled about that. It had taken me all my life to decide I wanted to search, and I wanted to do it now. I was patient, nonetheless, until it was almost a year. Then I started walking in to the Children's Aid Society and asking, "What's going on?" I began to make my presence felt — some workers would even recognize my voice when they picked up the phone. I'd also send them nice letters saying, "I know that you're swamped, but if you'd work as fast as you can, I'd really appreciate it." You know, play the game.

Pat, my birth mother, had been involved in Parent Finders, and I had heard a program about them two months before I met her. I'd written their number down and phoned it twice, but there was an answering machine, and I just felt it was too impersonal to leave any kind of message. So that number sat on my window-sill, and I could have met her earlier if I'd contacted Parent Finders.

So I waited and waited. Finally I got a registered letter in the mail saying the CAS had made contact with my birth mother and I'd have to wait a couple more weeks for the processing to be done. By now I was getting really impatient. I went right down there with the letter and said, "You're telling me a couple of weeks. Why?" They said it was due to paperwork and red tape, which is understandable. When I had to come down for my mandatory counselling at the CAS, to smooth it over in case the reunion didn't go well, I was at the point where I wanted to find her and for them to have nothing to do with it. I didn't come straight out and say that. We talked for almost two hours; I did most of the talking. I got her first name out of them, and then later on in the conversation a social worker slipped and said that my birth mother was involved in Parent Finders. The second she said that I looked at my watch and said, "Well, I have to go now." I went home, phoned Parent Finders and gave them my name and my birth mother's first name, Pat.

In a couple of hours I got a phone call saying they knew who my mother was and that she was on the other line. Did I want them to give her my phone number? I said, "Sure, let's do it!" Then she phoned me up and we talked for four hours on the phone. She had millions of questions, more than I did.

Pat is an amazing lady. She'd been obsessed with finding me. She'd been on TV, in newspaper articles, taken out ads in the classifieds, and she'd taken Children's Aid to court to try to get them to release my name.

When Abbigale Patterson embarked upon her search, she first told her adoptive father, who warned her to be prepared for whatever she found. Abbigale was able to acquire some general information from Halifax Social Services, but was shocked to hear that her birth father's identity was not confirmed:

When I read the part about his identity not being confirmed, I remember being very angry. I threw the letter across the room and yelled, "Slut!"

I had grown up all these years thinking my birth mother had been very innocent and had been put in a very awkward situation. Now I found out that she didn't even know who my father was. Obviously she'd been sleeping around. I was indignant and upset. I hated her, even though I'd always been grateful that she carried me, did not abort me, and gave me up for a better life. Well, now I believed that she had no choice. Her family probably wouldn't want her illegitimate child, and she had nowhere else to turn.

I was so angry with her that I finally told my adoptive mother. I explained that I didn't want her to be hurt by my search and that I just wanted to see my natural mother or find out what she or my father were like, so that I could look at them and see where I came from. My mother is great! She was understanding and loving. She accepted my need to know my natural mother.

But when I told her what I felt, how this woman wasn't the saint and the loving, kind person I'd always dreamed she'd be, she told me I was being too hard on her. She explained that I didn't know her circumstances and I shouldn't be so quick to judge her. Suddenly the words my father had spoken came rushing back to me. I realized I had not prepared myself.

Some time went by, and I hadn't lost interest in finding her, but my need wasn't quite as strong. I gradually came to believe that, yes, in fact, she did do the best thing for me and probably for her too at that time in her life. I began to forgive her. I even thought that sometime in the future I would try to find her again.

When a search leads to a birth parent who does not want contact, it can be devastating for the adoptee, a tearing open of the original wound, as it was for Leona Darling:

A couple of months after placing my name on the register, I was called in to see a social worker who gave me nonidentifying information. This was very limited, and she also told me that no one else in my family was registered. My father, it was stated, had doubts about whether or not he was the father of my brother and myself. Rejected again!

After I had told the social worker how I resented the fact that my parents had given me up and how I had absolutely no interest in meeting them, she did try to talk me into feeling some sympathy for my mother. I did understand my mother's predicament, but deep down I had absolutely no sympathy for her. I felt rejected and resentful.

I must tell you I am a very strong-willed person and I believe that anyone can do anything they want to if they put their mind to it, so I truly cannot understand how a mother could give up her own children. I felt that my mother was just being weak and giving in to her weakness and that if she had just tried harder she could have coped. Unreasonable, aren't I?

Tess Purvey also had her illusions destroyed by the rejection she encountered:

I had always known I was adopted, but was never permitted to discuss this outside the family. Subconsciously I had always wanted to know more, but my loyalty to my family delayed my acknowledgement of this. After thirty-three years and three children my need to know more about my roots overtook my sense of loyalty, and changes to the New Zealand laws enabled me to apply for my original birth certificate.

Four and a half years ago I received my certificate and began my search for my birth mother. Within forty-eight hours I was able to locate her. I decided that the best method of contact, for me, was to write to her.

Within two days of receiving my letter she phoned me. The initial conversation was brief, with a view to meeting in the near future.

I waited a further two years with no contact because I didn't wish to disrupt her life, but there were so many unanswered questions. My next step was to locate her place of work. Against my better judgement I decided to make a second attempt at contact, through a friend. We went to her place of work, and my friend went in and spoke with her, explaining that I was there. She didn't want to see me but promised to phone me that evening. Three days later she hadn't called, and in my heart, I knew she wanted nothing to do with me.

But I still needed to know who my father was. I asked my friend to phone and make sure she was all right. Two days later I received an extremely angry and unpleasant call from my birth mother. I managed to get my father's name but was told he had died during her pregnancy, in a motorbike accident. For eighteen months I searched for David and could find no record of him having been born in New Zealand, let alone having died here. I began to search in Australia and could get no leads there either. I had had contact by phone with one of my half brothers by this time and had received a very terse phone call from my birth mother telling me to leave all the family alone and to have no further contact with her. So, when I made one last contact with my birth mother it was nerve-racking to say the least. I formulated very specific questions, and I got the answers — I had been searching for the wrong person.

Sara Minchin was relinquished for adoption even though her birth parents were married. They already had a son and did not feel they could afford to give another child the education they would like. Although Sara has met her brother and has a good relationship with him, her birth parents live in South Africa, and she has yet to meet them:

I wrote to them for about a year and a half; however, I could never forget the fact that they had given me away and kept another child and had hardly been destitute as I saw it. I couldn't possibly understand how anyone could part with their child when they didn't have to.

In the end I felt I couldn't communicate with them anymore. I thanked them very much for all they had sent me but said that I couldn't come to terms with the fact that they had kept one child but had given me away. They seem to be rather hard individuals who don't appear to care about anyone but themselves. It makes you realize that it is the person who brings you up who shapes how you think, and you have their values and standards.

I am very glad I searched because I needed to know. I still have a great longing to see my natural parents in the flesh.

After a long search, Mary Powell used an intermediary to make first contact with her birth mother Phyllis:

She called and had a gruff reception from a male. She tried again, and Phyllis admitted she knew who Wendie was speaking about and listened for an hour. She said she couldn't make contact with me at this point in her life and refused to give me her medical history.

I was ecstatic, elated, nauseous and deflated. I don't wish to destroy her marriage or family, yet I want to meet her, hug her for allowing me to live, and introduce her to her beautiful granddaughters. I don't want to take over her life.

Diane Morris found her mother two years ago:

I wrote her a letter. It just said, "It was 1947 when I last saw you . . ." and a few little things like that. I sounded like a friend. I sent it to her home where she was living with her third husband. Just about this time she left her third husband. The letter got to her husband. He read it and gave it to his divorce lawyer to see if he could get any money from me. He had taken her for everything she had.

She went to live with my brother. The letter eventually got to her, and she called me. I was getting calls all across the nation about searches, and one day I picked up the phone and a voice said, "This is Audrey."

I said, "Who?" and she said, "Audrey!"

I said, "Oh, Audrey!" We talked for a while, then we exchanged letters. Unfortunately she doesn't want to meet me, though she still writes. She won't even tell her sister, who was with her when she was pregnant with me, that I've surfaced, and she sees her sister every day.

I want to meet her, but I haven't pressured her. She has gone through such a difficult time, such a rough divorce. Everything she had is gone. So we just write back and forth. I have a sister and two brothers, and none of them knows about my existence. I'm her daughter, and she acknowledges that fact, but if you ask she will say, "I have one daughter and two sons," not two daughters. I'm really not part of the family. I'm a pen pal.

Their family has a reunion every summer and she has mentioned in her letter that "everyone will be there." But I haven't been invited.

Janice Raymen found her mother within hours of starting her search. Despite this early success, the ending was far from what she expected:

I found my birth mother within two days of my search and wrote to her, but received a nasty reply. While searching for her, I found she had been married before I was born and that I had three older stepsisters and that I was the outcome of an affair and, therefore, illegitimate. She remained with her husband after my birth and went on to have a son after, my stepbrother.

After I received her note I gave a lot of thought to whether or not to contact my stepsisters or stepbrother. I went through Social Services to do this and received a phone call from one of my stepsisters, while my mother stood by her side. After a long phone call, my sister wanted to remain in contact with me, although my birth had upset their own lives so much.

At this time my mother had separated from her husband. Two days later she phoned and told me never to make further contact with any of her family. She has given me three different accounts as to who my father was, and although I have no name for him and am still trying to find out who he was, Social Services have told me my sisters will reconsider the situation when my mother dies.

The way this has affected me is that I live with it, I suppose you could say. Knowing you are rejected at birth is something you live with, but being rejected a second time is something very different. Even though I am part of them they seem to think of me as an alien or a threat to their lives.

I now know that for me to have waited forty-two years before beginning my search was a good thing, as I had the support of my own family to carry me through. But part of me is still missing. I will always remain in hope and feel so sorry for them all. I believe in some ways I was the lucky one of the family to have been given away, but I'm sure if they had only known me for a few minutes they would have realized I was different. I didn't wish to take anything from them, only to give.

Angela Netley's adoptive mother was a very cold person, which made her quest for a mother's love even more important to her:

I phoned my birth mother, and she was amazed I'd found her, was very friendly and asked me to phone again in a week. She said her husband and children already knew about me. But when I next called she handed the phone to her husband, who accused me of wanting money! I tried to convince him I was married, owned our own house and was to inherit from my late father's trust upon the death of my adoptive mother. He wouldn't listen. I then got a letter from his lawyer ordering me to have no contact. I tried to phone a couple of times, wrote to their minister, but all to no avail.

I felt it very badly — being rejected not once, but twice. Very painful. Now, at the age of fifty, I still feel it. I've always longed for the comforting arms of a mother. I could never, ever have parted with my two girls, and I've been married three times. I feel a sense of loss, am very insecure, but nevertheless, in spite of suicide attempts in the past, I have led a full, interesting life. I tend to "comfort" myself with food, which I have found other people who were adopted are prone to do.

I still feel bitter about my birth mother. What harm have I ever done her? I was a lovely baby, a pretty little girl and a beautiful teenager. So long ago, and yet it's still a big hurt. Why couldn't she have met me on halfway territory as we'd suggested? Isn't she curious even to glimpse me?

Sally Whiteside was twenty-nine when her adoptive father died. While sorting through his papers, she found something of great interest:

I found the court order giving the formal details of my adoption. Most importantly, I now knew the surname of my birth mother and where I was born. Because of the guilt directed towards my adoptive mother, it took me three years to send off for my original birth certificate. I then visited St. Catherine's House to gain further details. I was very lucky, for my natural grandmother, a widow, still lived at the same address as in 1957. It was therefore easy to find the phone number and make contact.

Initially my birth mother, Ann, felt unable to meet me. She had recently been ill and was too weak to talk to me. Also, her second husband didn't know about me, nor did her two children. However, I did meet my natural grandmother and uncle. They were pleased to see me, and we all hoped Ann would want to meet me eventually. My uncle said he had always known he had a niece out there and had been tempted to try to trace me. But Ann had always insisted on total secrecy because she was so frightened that her children would think badly of her.

After experiencing the intense joy that motherhood brought her, Jane Doe finally decided to act on the information she had and called her birth mother in Victoria:

I have made the decision. The phone call will take me to a different time zone. I can plan it to coincide with my daughter's afternoon nap tomorrow. It will be the day before my birthday. Perhaps this woman thinks about me at this time every year.

My home is quiet. Shaking fingers punch out the numbers. It is ringing all those miles away. What if she doesn't answer? What if she does?

"Hello?"

My God, her voice sounds just like mine! What am I going to say? "Is this Mrs. Smith? Mrs. Susan Jane Smith?"

"Yes, it is."

"Oh, uh, I . . . I . . . I don't know if you'll want to talk about this over the phone. Maybe I should write you a letter . . ."

"Who are you?" She sounds sharp, but almost friendly, inquisitive.

"I . . . I . . . You don't know me. I was born in 1955. My birthday is tomorrow."

There is no pause, just harshness. Her words come quickly: "I don't want to talk about it." Now she paused slightly and lowers her voice. "I mean, I don't know what you're talking about."

"Then I guess that's it."

"Yes, that's it." And she is gone.

I wonder what I am supposed to feel now. The truth is that I feel nothing. This nonconversation cannot change my life in any way. I will care for my family. I will continue to act the way people expect other people to act. I will work and I will talk to people and people will talk to me. It's easy. I will be a nice person, and I will do useful things.

And tomorrow some of my friends will be taking me out for a dinner to celebrate my birthday.

It has been estimated that, once contacted, ten to fifteen percent of birth mothers choose not to meet with their offspring. Arlene Nelson has been able to face this reality, one of the greatest fears of a searching adoptee, and turn it into a positive experience:

My mother has chosen not to meet me. However, she has opened the doors so I may be in contact with the rest of my biological family. Although we have only had our first meeting, my sister and three brothers were very welcoming. I was surprised by their interest and sense of responsibility.

Thank you to my mother for not cutting me off from the others. Now I have a better understanding and respect of my mother's situation.

Don Hunkin delayed his search until he had reached a certain level of self-fulfilment. He wanted to solve some of his problems of neediness without foisting them upon his birth parents:

The Adoption Disclosure Registry wrote that they could search for only one birth parent at a time, so I had to decide which one to search for. My birth father had written my adoptive mother a letter soon after my adoption. He had expressed sadness about the adoption and regret that he was unable to look after me himself. On the strength of this letter, I decided to search for him.

I had two purposes in searching for my father. The first was to let him know that I had survived and was happy with my life. The second was to give him the opportunity to resolve any incompleteness he might feel about me before he died. I imagined that by this time he would be in his mid- to late-seventies.

Almost exactly two years later the search began and was over within two weeks. My birth father lived in Vancouver and had agreed to a possible reunion. The Children's Aid Societies in our respective cities took over the case. We went through a counselling process, exchanging general information through caseworkers. This was painful for him as he had never expected to think about it again. There was also some concern about what I expected from him. I explained my motives in a letter, and satisfied, he signed the release that would allow direct contact.

Our first contact was by telephone, with a calling time arranged through Children's Aid. The thought occurred to me that he might be destitute and expect me to look after him. I had done what I could to take care of my own neediness, but had completely overlooked the possibility of his. As I was about to dial, the phone rang. Children's Aid had arranged that I would call, but he had decided to call first.

The conversation was very comfortable and easy, and after a brief synopsis of the past forty-five years, the conversation fell onto current topics. He turned out to be a salt-of-the-earth character, self-educated, a fervent socialist, a singer and generally satisfied with his life. I asked him about my adoption, medical history, family history and volunteered lots of information about myself. We talked for about an hour and a half, ending with an agreement to talk again the following Sunday, which we did. Since then we've had no contact, and this feels appropriate. I have friends living in Vancouver, and if I visit them I will probably get in touch with him.

I have never initiated a search for my mother. I'm indifferent about her, and if there is something preventing me from being interested, it is buried deeply and perhaps will surface later.

All considered, the preparation for searching has been more important to me than the actual finding. My intention to approach my birth father without expectation or demand allowed me to resolve much of the anger and sadness that had coloured every aspect of my life. The circumstances of my life — adoption, family dysfunction, search for my birth father — have proven invaluable in developing my appreciation of life. I'm grateful for them all.

While some adoptees must face the agony of a "second rejection," others endure the frustration of finding no trace of their parent. Sharon Leamy has suffered six and a half years of searching unsuccessfully for her birth mother:

Sometimes adoptees suffer from rejection and/or abandonment without realizing what is causing the pain. They can suffer insecurities in their relationships that can cause great damage. Until they can figure out why they feel the way they do, they cannot heal. I was finally able to come to grips with what was causing me to feel so insecure in my relationships. I have a hard time accepting that anyone could love me, and when they do, I test them to the limit. It's not something I do on purpose. If I knew I had been doing this, I might have been able to save my marriage. I now know that I don't have to feel this way. I do belong, and I have the right to be loved. I still need to heal the feeling of rejection.

In order for one to heal, one must be able to own the pain of the hurt — in my case, come to grips with the fact that I was put up for adoption and feel that I wasn't wanted. Next I have to accept the loss. The fact that I was taken away from my natural mother and my sense of belonging was taken away from me. Finally, I need to release the offender — my mother, who caused this pain by giving me up.

I cannot do any of these things without my birth mother, but I cannot find her because the legal system will not release any pertinent information to me. I am left to dangle, trying to piece together my birth like a murder mystery. Unfortunately the system will not help me, and the only way it ever will is if I stand up and say this is wrong and we have to change it.

If I ever find her, I am going to tell her how much I love her. I don't know her by sight, but I know her well in my heart, because she is the core of my existence.

Occasionally, a search may reveal adoption practices that are illegal in the West, although not uncommon in some countries with poor human rights records. These present unexpected problems. When helping her husband Frank locate his roots, Deborah Carrière found that their quest was to take them on a long and mysterious journey that began in London, Ontario:

In May or June 1991 we found a listing in East Germany for his birth sister. Frank spoke to a man representing himself as his sister's husband. As he knew who my husband was and the details surrounding the adoption, we accepted what he told us as true, that being:

1. Frank's birth mother had died.
2. His sister was in some sort of psychiatric hospital and was either unwilling or unable to speak.
3. His birth father had disappeared.
4. His uncle had disappeared.
5. All his blood relatives had disappeared, with one notable exception — his grandfather had been executed after the war for war crimes.

But in December 1991, Frank called his sister's number and was told that the government office had been closed. Further investigation revealed that he had been speaking before to a man from East Germany's infamous Internal Affairs Office, the secret police known as the Stasi.

We are still unable to determine why they knew so much about my husband. Needless to say we are unable to accept their information as true.

Initially we searched out of curiosity, then for medical information, but now the reason is to make sure Frank's birth family is all right and to tell them that my husband is fine. He was not voluntarily given up for adoption. I would say he was taken, as opposed to given.

Although he will continue to search for as long as it takes, the extraordinary circumstances of Joe Soll's adoption make it extremely difficult to trace his birth family:

I started my search and quickly found out I was sold by someone who'd sold almost five thousand babies over twenty years. This woman, Bessie Bernard, brought babies into New York from all over the East Coast, from Florida, Delaware, Massachusetts, Connecticut and from New York itself (never New Jersey, for some reason). She changed birth dates, birth names. I won a court case in which I sued for my records and got them, but my original birth certificate was altered. Everything the court has is false; there are no other papers. My birth certificate says I was born in the Broad Street Hospital in New York, and they said they never had a maternity ward. I think my birth date might be October 27 instead of November 3.

And I could have been born in Florida, because one of Bessie's tricks was to bring babies up from there. She would advertise in the Miami Herald: "Loving couple wants to adopt child." A pregnant woman would see it, come to her, Bessie would take the baby, then she'd go looking for someone to sell the baby to. She'd bring the baby to New York, which is where most of her clients were. She had nurseries in several places in New York, which is where I was for a couple of weeks.

Bessie was arrested in 1949. When the police came, she threw her black book to her father, who was in his seventies but jumped out of the window and ran down the fire escape. Bessie jumped on the back of the nearest policeman and bit, kicked and scratched. And this woman weighed 240 pounds! The trial lasted about ten months, and she was sentenced to two years in prison, but they told her that if she paid a 2,500-dollar fine they'd let her go, and that's what happened. The judge said — and it was incongruous since he was letting her off prison — that it was the worst case of dealing in human flesh he'd ever encountered. She died about three years ago. I never got to meet her, and the only person I know who did killed herself.

I'm doing my work, but I may never find out. And that's the most uncomfortable thought I have in my mind, the thought of dying and not knowing. How can I leave when I don't know how I got here? It's very incomplete.

There is yet another form of disappointment for some adoptees, as Jamie Boswell explains:

When I completed my search I found that my birth mother had passed away. She used her illness, which was diabetes, to kill herself on my twenty-third birthday. I was twenty-five when I found this out. There was a lot of anger. I went into depression. I was told my birth mother just got tired of waiting. She didn't have any other children, she wasn't married, her mother was dead, and her father had abandoned her, and she didn't know where he was. So she basically had no one left, except my cousins and it really wasn't a close family. Perhaps she was waiting for me to find her and had just had enough waiting. She got me a birthday card and a present every year on my birthday. We weren't able to find them anywhere, so I don't know what happened to them, whether someone threw them out when they cleared out her stuff or what.

I was able to keep my fantasy mother when my birth mother passed away. I didn't have to deal with a person. I think that everyone who has a reunion, even though they might not know it, has to grieve because of the loss of their fantasy mother.

So why do so many adoptees battle against the odds and accept the possibility of such anguish at the end of their search? Lois Mandel found her birth grandmother first, then waited for three years for her to give her information on her birth mother, to no avail. Lois's grandmother never told her daughter that Lois was searching for her. So Lois took what information she got from other sources and had a social worker make that initial call to her birth mother:

My mother was thrilled. In fact she told me that the night she got the phone call she had picked up an application for registration!

Alan Davidson has recently located his seventy-six-year-old birth mother. Although they have yet to meet, they have talked once on the phone, and Alan feels a lot of blank spaces in his life have been filled:

I felt totally different after our conversation. I felt warmer and calmer inside. My wife said I looked different! To learn who you are after all these years of wondering is indeed a huge relief.

8

The Search Is Over

It was so lovely and natural I almost
fell in love with her.

Josephine Richards

*T*HE END OF AN ADOPTEE'*s search is often sudden. A telephone*
call from a search agency may overturn the normality of life,
and searchers describe experiencing powerful, conflicting
emotions — excitement, anxiety, nervousness, shock, fear, joy.
There are sleepless nights before the reunion. For many, finally
meeting their birth parent or sibling is the healing experience
they hoped for. Family resemblances that others take for granted
become a source of wonder for both parties.

For others, the experience is the disappointment that a good
counsellor will have warned them they risk.

Because Rosemary Mackintosh's adoptive mother had been
abusive to her, she grew up with the fantasy that her birth mother
would be everyone's image of what a mother should be: "A
loving person, plump, with white hair tied back in a bun." Then
they met:

When she opened the door to me, I was met by a glamorous
blonde. My fantasy was shattered immediately. "Just call me
Margaret. After all, we're strangers," she said. Over tea she

began saying how she had been too young to keep me, that she didn't know who my father was, that she'd married a quite well-off businessman who didn't know of my existence and that she had four children. Her children and her husband were away; only thus was she able to see me. I told her I was married with a child. She showed no interest whatsoever.

After tea she phoned some friends, and I heard her ask, "Guess what I've got here?" and she began to chuckle. Within minutes three women arrived, and they all began to laugh. One woman walked right round me, gazing intently, then remarked, "Well, Margaret, your past has surely caught up with you." More guffaws. By this time I felt like a cow at a cattle market. When her cronies departed, my mother made it plain it was time I, too, went. She mumbled something about us meeting again. I knew as I waved goodbye from my taxi that she would never contact me again.

Thirty-two years have passed since that day, and I never saw or heard from her again. For a week after the visit I felt very upset, then I got on with my life without a chip on my shoulder at all, due to a very happy married life, I think. Now I can relate my story with a sense of humour and can honestly say, "All water under the bridge." For years I've never given my adoptive or real mother a second thought. I'm too happy with my own family.

As a mixed-race child living with a white family in the 1960s, it was obvious to Josephine Richards that she had been adopted. She was told that her birth mother had been seventeen when she was born and that she had been adopted when she was eighteen months old:

When I reached twenty-four, just before my own marriage, I decided to trace my mum. We managed to trace her quite quickly over a number of weeks. The social worker contacted my birth mother by telephone to explain the situation, and a few weeks later I wrote to her with photos, as if I was a long-lost friend.

She wrote back, and this carried on for a couple of weeks until she asked to visit me.

On the day I was really nervous, and when she knocked on the door she was not at all as I had imagined. We didn't kiss or hug and were very matter-of-fact. We were joined by her husband, who I later found out was the real reason that I had been adopted — either him or me! At the end of our chat this caused a slight disagreement, as my mother argued with him that I had every right to meet her, whilst he disagreed (although I thought he was a very nice person).

They went after an hour and came back that afternoon. But the lovely touch was when my mum Margaret kissed me and said, "See you later." The second visit was great, and we got on well, apart from her husband's watchful, perhaps jealous eye, which he kept on us.

We met later in the week and were like sisters. The loveliest moment was when we were on our own and we hugged and kissed. It was so lovely and natural I almost fell in love with her. She was wonderful.

Having discovered that his mother had died before they could reunite, Jamie Boswell decided to track down his birth father:

I spoke to him on the phone about a year ago. I met him last October for the first time. He denied any possibility of being my birth father. We've met two more times since then, and we're progressing along at a slow pace. He hasn't accepted it, but he's thinking about taking a blood test. I'm not too dependent on his needs. I don't care if he wants a son or not. But he's got two daughters, aged five and three, who are my half sisters, which is nice.

When Maureen Dinner received a call from an Adoption Disclosure counsellor to say that her birth mother had been found, her initial elation was shortlived:

The bad news was that my birth mother was devastated that she had been located. She asked the counsellor if she could tell me that they couldn't find her. My birth mother was told when she gave me up for adoption that she would never see me again and to get on with her life. With the contact from the agency, she was experiencing all the feelings she had pushed away thirty years ago and was having difficulty coming to terms with a reunion. The counsellor suggested I write a letter to my mother through her and perhaps address some of my mother's concerns. I did, and it must have been one of the hardest things I ever did. Anyway, the letter must have worked because soon after my mother agreed to meet me.

She didn't give me much notice. Looking back it was just as well, since I hardly slept or thought about anything else that week. Getting ready for that meeting in Toronto at the Children's Aid Society was bizarre. I had to make a good impression. I wanted her to know that I had turned out okay, and I wanted her to be proud of me. I got a haircut, bought new clothes, cleaned the car and told everybody I met what was happening that weekend (I could hardly keep quiet about it).

My adoptive parents were also very excited for me. They knew that this was something I had wanted for a long, long time. We spoke almost every day beforehand with each new development.

The morning of the meeting I had intense butterflies. My hands were clammy, my heart was pounding, and I really couldn't believe this was the day I was going to meet my mother. I thought, What have I got myself into and can I get out of it? To say I was nervous would be an understatement.

I was about forty-five minutes early, so I thought I would park and try to spot her going into the building to get some idea of what she was like. Later I found out she was already there and had arrived a lot earlier than her scheduled time. She was to meet the social worker at the agency, and they would put her in the family room. I would then arrive and meet the social worker, and she would take me in to meet her.

As the worker and I approached the door, I told her to give me some warning as to when we were getting near so I could take a breath, but we were already there. The step I took into that room was probably the hardest one I've ever had to take.

Right away my mother came over and hugged me and held me and cried. Then we sat down and just stared at each other for a long time. I was struck that she didn't look like me. All my life I had pictured her as being just like me, except a little older. I'd brought some photos of me during childhood. She cried a lot looking at those and said it made her happy to see the things I had been exposed to (ballet classes, pets, siblings, etc.) but very sad, too.

My mother has much regret for what she did, relinquishing me. She feels very guilty for doing that to me. I tried to tell her that I am not bitter, that I had a really good life with wonderful parents who raised me and loved me and gave me a good home and a sister.

My mother was very open with me and told me she would tell me anything I wanted to know. I asked her what it was like being pregnant with me. It was great to be able finally to ask someone! She told me all about her doctor's appointments, when and where she went into labour, who took her to hospital, all about the labour and delivery, who came to visit her in the hospital and who drove her back to the maternity home after relinquishing me.

It has been a year since our first visit — a year of firsts: Christmas, birthdays, etc.

Jerry Appleton had grown up with adoptive parents he loved dearly. His mother's dying wish had been that he be happy, and finding his birth mother would, he knew, satisfy her desire. After a search for his birth mother that had taken him across Canada,

he finally obtained her phone number. Anxious to approach a
reunion in the proper way, he contacted a psychiatrist with the
Children's Aid Society before making the next move:

I said, "This is where I'm at. This is what I think I must do."
The person spent an hour with me on the phone, confirming that
everything I was wanting to do was just commonsense and
caution.

I got on a plane and flew to Victoria, and checked into a hotel.
For two days I practised dialling my mother's phone number and
hanging up, I was so frightened. I didn't know what to say to
her. Finally, the second day, I got slower at the process, and
suddenly before hanging up, I heard my mother's voice. I said I
was Jerry Appleton from Cornwall, and I had been given her
phone number and told to call her if I ever I was in Victoria. We
talked about nothing, and at one point, this lady, who had no
idea who was on the phone to her, said probably the most
touching phrase she could have said to me: "You sound like a
wonderful young man. Why don't we have tea tomorrow?" I
thought, Over tea I'll tell her. How civilized.

Then she asked me the question I feared the most, because I'd
promised myself a long time ago that I wouldn't lie about it. She
said, "You know, I don't know anyone named Appleton. How
did you come to call me? How are we connected?"

I didn't know what to say. I paused and said, "Does the name
Caron mean anything to you?" Many years before I had found
out my birth father's last name.

There was a long pause, and all she said was, "Tea tomorrow
at ten."

She arrived the next morning. She looked frightened, and she
was clutching a little plastic bag. She sat down and clutched the
bag so tightly. For about fifteen minutes we talked about the
mountains, the ocean, the city and then, out of pure instinct, I
did something I'd never been allowed to do. I was a little boy

to my mother so in a little-boy voice I said, pointing to the plastic bag, "Something for me?" I was surprised. She smiled and said yes. She had bought me a shirt. It was ugly and two sizes too big, and I thought, It's supposed to be the prerogative of every mother to buy that wrong tie, wrong socks and wrong shirt.

We talked on for about ten minutes, then I did it again. I don't know what prompted me, but in a little-boy voice — exaggerated, with a giggle in it — I said, pointing to the bag. "Something else for me?"

She smiled and said yes. She said to me, "I brought pictures of your grandmother."

We sat there for eight hours. We giggled, laughed, cried a lot, hugged, and she told me the story I had waited a lifetime to hear. She told me, with great difficulty because she was hurting, about her life, about this gentleman whose name was Caron. I would stop her every once in a while and say, "You don't have to. I don't need to hear this," but she would say, "You don't understand. I need to say it."

She had never told anyone. When she became pregnant, the soldier had left for further training and then been sent overseas. She went to Ottawa when she found out she was pregnant, and discovered that the soldier had been killed. I remember her telling me, with enormous tears in her eyes, that, after she had given me up and I'd been placed in an orphanage, she went home and wrote the soldier a letter, despite the fact that she knew he was dead. She mailed it, thinking it was good for her soul. In the letter she simply said what she had now told me, that the child was born, that she had given him the name Brian Moore and that the child had been placed in an orphanage. And she went on with her life.

None of her family or friends knew about the child. Later, she married; they had no children, and she never told him. I couldn't share her life openly. I understood that because that was one of the possibilities I was told to expect, that it might have been such a secret that she might have a life and a family I couldn't share.

As time passed, I found the family of this dead soldier. I found an enormous pool of family love that I really had never known. He had actually been seriously wounded in the war, come back, got married, had two daughters and then had died prematurely.

What I found out later was that my birth mother had had two sons, one born thirteen months before me from another father. I had unknowingly deceived her by bringing her the wrong information. I was given information that my father was Caron a long time ago, but he wasn't. When I had gone to the Children's Aid Society they wouldn't tell me anything, but they glanced into the file. Unknowingly, they weren't looking in my file but my brother's — he was born in the same hostel and to the same mother — an innocent, stupid mistake. So I had arrived with the wrong father's name, and my birth mother naturally assumed I was that child. I still don't know who my birth father is. I'm still searching.

Despite the emotional and physical bond between them, the birth mother and adoptee are strangers at the moment of meeting.

Throughout Jan Rourke's search she had been questioning whether any good would come out of the experience. After their reunion, when she and her birth mother Josie were alone in her car afterwards, she received her answer:

Josie then became quiet, almost as though she was trying to work out how to bring up the question on her mind. Then she finally asked: Did I hate her for what she'd done to me? How I kept from driving off the road I will never know. She'd somehow come to the conclusion that I must have felt some animosity or even hatred towards her for abandoning me as an infant.

In the entire range of emotions I ever experienced when thinking and wondering about my biological mother, those two had never entered my mind. Gratitude, appreciation and even some sympathy would be more accurate. How can anyone feel anything else towards a woman who made the ultimate sacrifice for the good of her child? She had had the courage and faith to believe that someone else would be able to offer me the things she couldn't and gave me over to another to raise. That act meant I was lucky enough to be raised by the best mother and father anywhere. I hope I would be able to be as selfless if I was ever in the same position, but somehow I doubt I could.

When I told Josie this, and that I would always be grateful to her for the courage it must have taken, the sense of relief within the car was almost a physical presence. I hadn't been aware of a barrier between us, but I was suddenly aware of its absence.

Steve Tobis remembers suffering through great anxiety as he sat in a social worker's office waiting for his first meeting with his birth mother:

I was sweating and thinking, Oh, my God, what's going to happen now? I was nervous but I looked cool, calm and collected. Because of the way I was brought up it was very difficult for me to show emotions. My adoptive parents weren't loving; all they did was argue. The only thing I learned from my father was how to work. Suddenly there she was. She said, "That's my son." I didn't share her emotions. We hugged. I was distant. I hugged her because that's what I thought I should do, not because I felt it or wanted to. Today I can hold her and kiss her and love her because I know she's my mother and I know what a wonderful person she is. But at that moment, this woman was still a complete stranger to me.

We sat down on the couch, and she asked, "What have you done with your life? Who are you?" because she didn't really know. We talked; first of all I found out what her maiden name was — Katzman. I asked, "Am I related to Howard Katzman?"

and she said, "Yes, he's our cousin." I played cards with him every Tuesday night!

She asked, "What kind of work have you done? What's your profession?" I said I was an entrepreneur and that I owned an ice-cream business for about ten years.

She said, "You have a cousin who does that; maybe you know him — Sid Barrish." He was my competitor! We knew each other through business because we were arch enemies, at each other's throats. I couldn't believe it; all these things were so coincidental. Then I found out that one of my brothers had lived a half block from me for two years.

All Karen McKenzie knew about her birth parents was that her mother had had an affair with a married man with two children. She registered with her local Children's Aid Society, but it brought no luck, so she went back to her busy life and gave it no more thought:

I always knew I was adopted. I had a little curiosity, but not much else until I had my own children. My four daughters all look like each other, and it was fascinating to me because I had never had anyone look like me before.

The phone rang on October 4, 1988, and it was a local social worker telling me my full birth brother had registered and wanted to meet me. Since I had not been told I had other siblings besides the ones my birth father had, I was in shock.

That morning was a rollercoaster for me. I went through every emotion: elation that I had a brother, wonderment that someone was looking for me, anger that no one had told me I had a brother and over the loss of the years we could have had together, anxiety that he would accept me as myself and fear that he would want something from me I couldn't give.

When I met my brother Jim we hugged and cried and started talking, a little awkwardly at first, but later went back to his house and talked for hours. When I left at about 11 pm, I was drained. Also, at the time of our reunion our worker had told us there appeared to be more siblings! We learned our birth mother had had seven children, six with the same man! It was an overwhelming day, full of information, and it has taken a long time to take it all in.

After Steve Tobis's initial reunion with his birth mother Rishy, they decided to meet for lunch:

It was very unusual because her husband Sam, my father now, came with us. I couldn't talk to Mom; the conversation was mainly between me and Dad. I felt more comfortable talking to a man than I did my mother.

She made me feel nervous; I was uncomfortable, uneasy. I wasn't myself. The other reason why I was being distant from her was that I already had a mother. My adoptive mother was the one who raised me, she was there when I was sick and when I was growing up. She was also there to fight and argue with. To put it on a scale, I'd say there was more bad than good about my adoptive mother. But she was there, and to me that's what a mother was. I didn't need another one.

I had no idea where it would lead, what was going to grow; if we would meet and that would be it, thank you very much and goodbye. So I was talking to them like I would talk to two people at a party who I'd just met for the first time. I was being standoffish, very distant.

We made a deal at the lunch table that we wouldn't tell anyone about our meeting. I didn't want anyone from my family to know, and Rishy didn't want anyone from her family to know until she had told her father after Passover.

Paul Patterson had found his birth mother and spent hours with her on the phone. Now a face-to-face meeting was about to take place:

She said, "I'm going to be there shortly. I'm the fat lady in a white car," and I said, "I'll be the skinny guy standing out there with brown hair." Sure enough she came and we hugged. We kept looking at each other. Then we went out to dinner for three hours; then back to my place and talked until about six o'clock in the morning.

I didn't see so much a physical resemblance as one of personality. It was incredible and really scary, actually. Our personalities are really, really close — I'm amazed. I'm sure there are a lot more genetic connections than people have any idea about. It would have been different if I'd been raised by her; then you would think it was more of an environmental thing.

We did a little investigation work to find my birth father. Pat had seen him for a couple of months; he knew about my birth, and he gave his nonidentifying information. That was the extent of it. Pat remembered where he'd been living with his parents, so we went there, but they weren't living there anymore. We knocked on the neighbours' doors; no one seemed to know much, but one guy said he thought he'd moved to Vancouver. Then we went to the public library, and sure enough, there was his name in the Vancouver phone book. I phoned him for about a month, but he was in California doing some business, so we weren't even sure it was him. Finally, one night, we called and he was there. Pat talked to him a bit and said, "There is someone here who wants to talk to you. Your son." He took it well, although I know it shocked him. Within thirty days I went out there with my girlfriend and met him. It was very interesting; there were a lot of similarities there as well. He looks more like me than Pat does.

I met my girlfriend at Parent Finders. She's adopted as well, and she does searches, for nothing, out of the goodness of her heart. She has the same attitude I do — that adoptees should have more rights. Every adoptee deserves to know who brought them onto this planet; I don't think that's asking too much. She said that if I wanted help finding my dad she was eager to help me. I phoned her up the next day, and we went out for dinner, and that was it — from that day on it's just been an amazing relationship. I'd never been out with an adopted person before, and we have so much in common. I'd only known her for two months, and she came out to Vancouver with me and met my father.

Meeting Pat has dramatically affected my life. It's a complete turnaround, very psychologically healing. I know who I am now. I wanted to meet my birth parents even if I didn't like them. You don't have to. It leads to an understanding of who you are. I love Pat now, but if you'd asked that question right after I met her, I wouldn't have known how to answer. It's been really strange because she has this urge to mother me, but I'm a little bit old for that.

After we met there were moments when we would argue. Since I moved in with her there have been times when I left for a week and came back. We had a lot of nights of staying up until six o'clock in the morning with a lot of tears. She feels guilty and was psychologically damaged by giving me up. It really, really caused an upset in her life. A lot of times it would upset me because she would focus on the pain she experienced, not my pain. It was like a power play — who grieved the most?

After the reunion with his birth mother, Steve Tobis asked her to help him locate his birth father. She procrastinated but finally gave him the phone number:

I got up enough nerve and called. I asked for Stan, and the person who answered wanted to know who I was and said if I didn't identify myself they wouldn't let me speak to him. I said, "Okay, idiot, I'm his son."

The guy said, "Oh, no, another one? The old man sure got around!"

When I got in touch with him I said, "Stan, you don't know me, but I'm your son. You went out with a girl named Rishy and got her pregnant, and I'm your son and would like to met you."

He said, "I never knew."

We arranged a time to meet, and I met him. He brought his daughter for moral support. He didn't look anything like the picture I saw from 1954. As soon as his daughter saw me she said, "That's your son. You can tell; he looks like my other brother."

We talked for a while, but all he did was just sit there and say, "I didn't know, I didn't know." His hands were shaking; you could tell he was nervous. I was very uncomfortable.

It was a very short meeting, maybe an hour or so. I said, "I'll give you a call sometime, and maybe we'll go out for a drink." He said that was a good idea.

Bonnie Robertson had filled out the necessary forms and was ready to begin her search on the day she turned eighteen. The Children's Aid Society was able to find a match, so she set out with her counsellor to meet her birth mother:

We were sitting in the restaurant discussing what was about to happen, my back to the entrance, when my worker said, "I think she's here." I took a deep breath and waited . . . then there she was, standing right beside me. We looked at each other, and we hugged and cried, giggled, cried and hugged some more. It was overwhelming, yet I was so happy that this day had finally come.

Charlene and I talked and laughed and cried some more. At one point she said that I had asked so many questions, but she couldn't understand one thing — I hadn't asked her why. I told her that I already knew why. I had understood for a long time that she had made the right decision. Charlene seemed almost amazed. I know that my understanding of her situation was due to the openness and support of my parents. They had always told me that this woman loved me dearly, and I knew it.

Leona Darling's birth brother could not wait to go through proper channels to meet her. Instead, once he found out her first name he found a way to contact her directly:

My name is uncommon, and his boss happened to be an old boyfriend of mine and knew I had been adopted (small world, isn't it?). My brother put two and two together and took a chance in trying to contact me, hoping I was the right person.

He then proceeded to tell me that we already knew each other, that he had been married to the daughter of a friend of my husband. It all clicked. I did remember meeting him thirty years ago. It felt very strange, his being someone I had known and not realizing we were brother and sister. Thank God we never dated!

We couldn't hear enough about each other and arranged that he would come to my home on Friday morning for us to meet. Of course, I didn't sleep for the next two nights and was unable to concentrate on anything. My family and friends all thought I was hilarious, walking around in a daze with this huge grin on my face.

I didn't want anyone else around when we met, so everyone else was away from the house when he arrived. I was very nervous until he arrived and then became very calm. He was very nervous and emotional. In fact, this reunion appeared to be much more important to him than to me.

After that meeting with my brother, we talked on the phone frequently. Our phone bills were atrocious. Dave had had a very unhappy childhood with his adoptive family and was in an unhappy second marriage. He felt that meeting his family would change his life, and all his problems would be eliminated. I had no such expectations.

Dave and I have been very supportive of each other. He looks on me as someone he can trust completely and tell all his problems to. I have tried very hard to meet his expectations. I feel that we have no past history to get in the way of our relationship now. I sometimes wonder if we would be as close now if we had gone through all the ups and downs of growing up together. We have a common bond, having been the two children given up for adoption, when the others had been kept in the family.

Leona had always felt great resentment toward her birth mother, who had given up two of her children as a result of a difficult marriage. At first it was only her siblings she wanted to meet, but after her reunion with Dave she changed her mind:

I had a telephone call from Dave stating that he was just leaving to go to visit our mother and that they had just spoken on the phone. I told him he'd better pick me up on the way because I was going, too. It seems I just needed my mother to indicate that she wanted to see us for me to change my mind about meeting her. (Not rejected anymore?)

If you ever wanted to see a nervous wreck, I was it. I was in a terrible state. Anyway, we finally arrived, and for once in my life I was at a loss for words. I couldn't speak. I didn't know what to say. What do you say to your mother when you haven't seen her for fifty years?

I just stared at her. The poor woman mustn't have known what to do. She did give us a hug and cried a little. We stayed for a couple of hours, and she told us about family members and showed us pictures. I suppose it was because of nervousness that she didn't ask us much about ourselves and instead talked on incessantly about herself and about her grandchildren and her daughter who had died the previous year.

Before we left a couple of hours later, Dave asked her if he could call her Mother. She said she would like that and turned to me and said that I could call her Mother also. I instantly said I couldn't do that as I already had a mother. She said she could understand that and it would be all right if I wanted to call her by her first name.

I left that evening feeling a little disappointed that she didn't show much interest in us, our interests or our families, her grandchildren. I felt she was a bit self-centred and that I would have to give a great deal of thought to whether I would want to develop a relationship with her or not.

But within a couple of weeks of our first visit, I decided to spend the day with her and try to get to know her better. That visit went much better. I gently told her what my feelings had always been towards her but how that had changed when she agreed to meet us. I also told her that I hoped we could start to get to know each other and become friends. She seemed very pleased by this.

She and I are very much alike. We don't look at all alike, but we have the same talents and have a lot of the same likes, dislikes and opinions on things. In fact, we get along quite well. We talk on the phone, and I try to visit her about once a month. However, I still find it difficult to think of these people as my family. I think it is due to my age and that my adoptive family were all I had for so many years.

Diana Lintott, who searched for her birth mother for seventeen years, now helps others find their roots. In her experience, ninety to ninety-five percent of reunions are considered successful by those involved, and hers, fortunately, also fitted into that category:

In some ways the reunion was like a dream. My birth mother asked me to bring along baby photos of myself. The first thing she did was compare them with the photo of me she had carried for forty years. This seemed to satisfy her that I was her daughter. Throughout our conversation she kept referring to me as "she" instead of "you," a sign perhaps that it took time to realize I was the baby she gave up so long ago.

Most important, my birth mother answered the questions that had haunted me for so long. She said she had screamed when she had to sign the papers releasing me for adoption and that the social worker had to tear me from her arms. But, being only eighteen years old, she had had little choice. Before the weekend was over, my birth mother had met my adoptive mother. I think that satisfied something in all our lives.

I'm so glad I didn't put my search off any longer. My birth mother died in 1986. I have so many memories I treasure, and I'm glad I had the privilege of meeting her. My adoptive mother also died just a year later. I'm so glad they met.

Since I've found my family, I've been working as a volunteer with Parent Finders in Edmonton as a search consultant, helping others find their families and gain the same satisfaction. I've heard from almost two hundred searchers who have completed their searches. I've witnessed a change in these adoptees, one of contentment and the satisfaction of knowing who they are and feeling they are a part of this world. It's a very rewarding and worthwhile part of my life.

This is a story that's just starting. The end of my search has made my life more complete. I have roots, just like everyone else!

9

I Need to Say I'm Sorry

My biggest fear is that you may despise
me for giving you up.

Patty Stover

*T*HE END OF THE SEARCH *is often equally sudden for the birth parent as it is for the adoptee, and brings a similar rush of conflicting emotions. For parents, however, there is often the additional fear that they will be confronted with accusations and blame; many express their need to explain themselves to their lost child, to gain understanding and forgiveness.*

Since the parent has no right to information and can often do little except register a willingness to be found, the news that the adoptee is within reach can cause shock and confusion even to those who have registered. When parents do attempt actively to trace their adopted children, they are likely to face more bureau-cratic red tape than adoptees, more incorrect information, more refusal.

Even when a search is successful and contact is made, the final reunion may not take place, for many reasons. Some parents may feel that meeting their child is not in the best interests of the adoptee at that time. Those who have not disclosed the secret to their families may fear that a reunion may threaten current relationships. Sometimes the adoptee is not willing, and the parent must be content with knowing, finally, that the child is well and happy.

Rishy Powell had never forgotten the son she had given up twenty years before, and although she was now married with a grown family she knew that she could not recover completely from the loss until she faced him again. After registering with various search groups she answered the telephone one day and received the news that her son was looking for her. Her reaction to the reality of meeting her child illustrates the confusion and apprehension many parents experience at this moment.

She asked me if I was okay and said to take my time, that she'd wait. Then she said, "Your son registered, and we've made a connection. You have a thirty-four-year-old son, a daughter-in-law from Australia and two granddaughters."

I said, "My cup runneth over! I can't believe it."

Steve grew up maybe three blocks away from where I lived!

The Adoption Research Foundation wanted me to come down for an interview; then they would interview my son and set up a reunion. When I went to the interview I was asked the history of my family. I told her straight away that if he was into drugs I couldn't meet him; it wouldn't be fair to my husband. When Steve was interviewed he said, "If they're Orthodox, forget it."

He had dropped some pictures off at the agency. When she showed them to me I couldn't make a connection with Steve. I said, "He's not my son. I don't believe it." I was expecting a blond, blue-eyed baby, but this was a dark-skinned man (he looks like me, but I didn't see me in the picture). She saw how upset I was and said, "What did you expect? You can't have your baby back. This is a thirty-four-year-old stranger." I started to cry. She said, "If you're that upset let's leave the reunion for a later time."

My kids didn't know anything about this yet. I called my sister and kids, told them briefly what had happened and asked them to come over. They couldn't get over how Steve looked like me. Then I said, "Look, I don't want to talk about this anymore. I don't care." I was angry with myself, angry for getting myself into this position in the first place and having to make a decision I didn't want to make. My son was expecting his parents to be the Rothschilds. I don't know what I was expecting; he just didn't seem like my kid. I said, "I'm going to go to that reunion on Monday, and I'm going to look into those eyes you say look so much like mine, and I'm going to see then if he's mine. If I can't make that connection, I just don't know."

Unlike Rishy, Jean Clark had not attempted to trace her child. She felt as if she had received a physical blow when she heard the news that her birth daughter had succeeded in finding her:

My first reaction was, Why? What's it going to prove? Why does she want to? What will it change for her even if I do see her? Then many things ran through my mind like, Oh my God, I'll lose my job; my husband will leave me. Really bizarre things — you must remember I had never forgiven myself. I went home and cried all night. I had to decide whether I would see this child, consider all the risks that went with it. How do I know if she's on drugs? How do I know if she's hated me all these years? How do I know, how do I know? Or do I run the risk within myself of rejecting her again. Remember I did once, twenty years ago.

The man that I work for is very observant. When I went to the office the next day he eventually got it out of me. He said, "Well, you can sit there with egg on your face or you can deal with it." He said, "You're going to need help with it."

So I went to a counsellor who was absolutely superb. She said, "Come in tomorrow morning at 8:30," so I did, and I talked until about 12:30.

I phoned the adoptive mother that afternoon, and I called Debbie that night. I told her who I was. I said, "I will see you, and I'm anxious to see you, but I need some time." I met her one week later.

Happily, the prospect of a reunion with their lost child brings immediate joy and excitement to many searching parents. It was a December evening when Micki Stocks read her horoscope in that day's newspaper: "Someone special enters your life, and it almost seems like a miracle." When she noticed a small ad in the personal column she knew her miracle had indeed arrived: "Adopted Son Looking for Birth Mother. Birth Name, Lorne. Born June 13, 1962, in Ontario. Please Call David at _____."

My heart stopped. I couldn't breathe! I thought for one fearful moment that I might be hallucinating. I put the paper down, walked into the bathroom to wash my hands and face . . . and then came back into the kitchen and picked up the paper again. *This* time when I saw the ad I burst into tears! My nineteen-year-old son ran into the kitchen asking what the problem was. When I pointed (sobbing and unable to talk) to the ad, he asked excitedly, "Is that him?" I could only nod; I was beyond words!

Later that evening I talked on the phone to my beloved firstborn for the very first time! My feelings of joy and happiness were indescribable! My search was over. We were both so excited on the phone that the words just kept tumbling out of us. We talked nonstop for almost an hour and a half. He told me, among other things, that he was six feet tall, had brown hair and brown eyes and had graduated in 1984 with a Bachelor of Commerce degree. He described himself as quite shy, but an avid reader and interested in sports. I wrote everything down as he told me. I wanted to know everything about him! I had a lot of catching up to do.

One day Debra Johnson received a surprise telephone call from her mother telling her she had received a letter with a number for her to telephone:

As I was listening, I was thinking, What is she saying to me? She started reading the letter to me, and my heart started racing. I could hardly think straight. I hung up the phone and phoned my husband at work right away. I said, "Tracey Lynn is trying to contact me."

He was just ecstatic. He said, "I knew it would happen." He was so excited. I sat on the bed for about half an hour with the phone in my hand, thinking, "What am I going to say? How am I going to say it?"

Thirty-six years before Shirley Carter had relinquished her son Paul. Now as she answered the telephone her past had become her present:

An investigator phoned me to say he was working for Paul and had been trying to find me. He suggested a meeting at his house with Paul on the Thursday. Oh . . . I never slept from the time I got the phone call to the Thursday. I didn't sleep, honestly. I went through every emotion possible in that week, waiting for the time of our meeting. I walked into that room, and there he was. The cheeky eyes were all there, and it was so emotional.

When a birth mother marries and has more children, she is reminded of the life she relinquished and of what she could have given her child if only she had been in better control of her life. She often has an overwhelming need to explain her situation at the time of the adoption, to see the child again and say how sorry she feels. Marilyn Hansen had borne a daughter, Katherine, in 1970 and kept this a secret for twenty years:

In 1972 I married. Our "first" child, a son, was born, and died at three days old. I never mentioned my actual first child, not even to my husband, and the death of our son seemed to me to be my punishment. I subsequently gave birth to two more sons.

I cherished these precious babies, and still do, every day. I also thought of Katherine every single day. I never stopped wondering. I never stopped hoping that one day we would connect. I always wondered if she was thinking of me, too.

On October 30, 1990, I got the telephone call I had hoped and prayed for. It was from Katherine's adoptive father. Using a tiny bit of information which they had jotted down twenty years before during discussions with the social worker, they had been able to track me down. Not wanting to intrude on my life, he was extremely cautious in his approach. I quickly assured him that I was thrilled and delighted. He said Katherine, now called Valerie, would be amazed and excited at how quickly contact had been established and how receptive I was. I talked with her adoptive mother and father for nearly two hours; we shared our lives with each other, hearing about twenty lost years. We decided they should call Valerie and advise her that contact had been made and let her call me when she was ready.

The phone rang about ten minutes later, and it was the most incredible experience. This was my baby girl. We cried and laughed and exchanged all sorts of information. It was the beginning of the most wonderful relationship.

Carole Jones had for years been regretting relinquishing her son for adoption. She was determined to find him once again to try to explain:

I wanted him to know where he came from and that he wasn't the product of a one-night stand with an unknown father; also that he wasn't given away because he was unloved and unwanted. He was very loved and very wanted, but I couldn't give him all the things a child should have, and I had learned these facts the hard way.

I had married at seventeen and separated at eighteen with a nine-month-old daughter. Then I had been in a two-year relationship with the father of my son, who had refused to marry me. My daughter was five years old and suffering from prejudice at school, not only from other children because she hadn't a father to talk about, but also from the attitude of parents and — to my dismay — teachers, who really should have known better. This was in 1966, and my daughter was the only one from a broken home.

When my son was twenty-one, my daughter undertook the search on my behalf. She contacted the Salvation Army, and they found him within three weeks. He contacted my daughter, and she was able to tell him that his birth mother was alive; that she had eventually married his father; that he now had a sister and brother and that we were all anxious to meet him. He lives two hundred miles away, so when he made his first visit he stayed four days with my daughter who is married with two daughters. That was four years ago, and we have been slowly getting to know each other. If I had known that I would eventually marry his father, I would never have let him go, but no one has a crystal ball.

Some parents, however, never retrieve the opportunity to befriend their estranged child. A long quest may sometimes end in sadness. Susan Baines had registered with NORCAP so that as soon as her birth daughter reached eighteen she would be easily traceable:

Over the years I would look at the photographs I had of Ann, her birth certificate, her adoption certificate and the lock of hair I had secretly taken from her. I always felt that I would see her again one day. I thought of her every year on her birthday. I wondered where she was, what she was like, if she was happy and what her mum and dad were like.

Eventually, in March 1991, I read an article on adoption which mentioned the name of a private tracing agency. I immediately contacted the lady, who was very sympathetic and kind.

In August she called to say that she had traced my daughter's family and was about to make contact. The day after, she rang to say that my daughter had been killed in 1980 after being hit by a car. She was on her way to school at the time.

I couldn't believe that this was true; I didn't want to believe it. In desperation I contacted the crematorium to find where she was laid to rest. I also contacted the court which had arranged the adoption. It was all true. I had lost my daughter twice.

I have written to her parents, and we have exchanged photographs, but they say they don't feel able to meet me at the moment. I feel very cheated and very empty. How I wish I had never had my baby adopted. That awful feeling of emptiness will never leave me.

Helen Kane (Buckton) was shocked when the adoptive parents of her child phoned her out of the blue. Although she had dreamed of finding her daughter, the news she heard was out of a nightmare:

I was surprised and perturbed by the news that my daughter had been in and out of mental hospitals and had spent time in prison for her disruptive behaviour and violent actions. I couldn't believe the things I was hearing. It was a complete shock. It sounded as if her adoptive parents were at the end of their tether and ready to give up after being through so much with their daughter. A million thoughts were running through my head and a million questions. Would she have been different if I had kept her?

The long-awaited reunion may not take place for other reasons. It takes two to make contact. Brenda Hobbs was elated when her social worker told her that her daughter had registered with the Children's Aid Society, too. She was hoping that this would be the year they could spend Dawn's birthday together. Brenda's dreams were shattered, however, when her daughter decided she did not want a reunion after all:

This experience has taken me once again down the long tunnel of depression; I've been re-examining my life and feelings of worthlessness. I am a practical, logical person who has always taken life in her stride, always understood the way things have to be, the way things are — always understanding the other person. This time, as much as I understand the difficulty my daughter is facing, I long for her to understand my feelings, understand my needs.

I want to stop grieving. I need to see my own flesh, to touch my offspring, to ease my pain. I want to know what she was like as a baby, a child, an adolescent, a teenager. What are her favourite things in life? What do we have in common? How do we differ? How can we help each other understand our situations and feelings if she won't come full circle?

Was her decision not to go further than a meeting with our counsellor made before she found out that I'm only a secretary, nobody special? I feel my insecurities mounting. I'm very pleased to know that my little girl landed on her feet. To know that Dawn has been safe all these years, has had a happy home and is continuing her education, working towards becoming a professional, eases the fears I've been harbouring about her well-being. That she cares enough for her adoptive mother not to want to upset her by acknowledging my existence tells me she is a caring individual. It hurts me as much as giving her up the first time; she has just slipped through my fingers for the second time. I feel like Alice tumbling down the rabbit hole — again. I keep reading the same book, but I never make it to the end.

When undertaking to unravel one's past, one must be prepared for disappointment. "Five years ago," says Judith Kizell-Brans, "I was still in denial. I would not even refer to my daughter by name, to myself." But Judith was able to come to terms with her decision and eventually locate her birth daughter, who does not want contact with her. It is difficult for Judith, but she says she has to respect the feelings of her daughter and her adoptive parents:

But the difference is I know where she is and I know she's alive. I have researched the family, and I know a lot about them. It's a good family. She's safe, and I know she wasn't abused, which for most birth mothers is the biggest fear they have.

When Patty Stover's search was coming to a close, before meeting her birth daughter she sent her the following letter:

I have a hundred questions whirling through my mind, as I am sure you have. I wonder what you have done for the past twenty-three years. Are you working or at university? Are you married? What are your parents like? Most of all I hope you are well and happy.

I am sure you wonder about your roots, who you look like and why I gave you up.

The most difficult and painful decision in my life was to relinquish all rights ever to see you or know about you again. Yet I justify my decision on the basis that I wanted you not to live a life of misery. I was only seventeen, still at school, and had no financial means to support us, nor did your birth father. If your birth father had been of a different nature, I would have married him. During the latter part of our relationship his behaviour changed drastically. All I could think about was that I didn't want you exposed to such unthinkable behaviour. I was just glad that on the day you were born two loving people would take you away and safely protect you.

Yet when you were born I was left with such a void. All the other mothers in the hospital were kissing, cuddling and feeding their babies, telling me I would regret my decision. I cried incessantly, wondering if I was doing the right thing. You were born in an era when unmarried, pregnant women were socially unacceptable. In the sixties you either went to a home or into hiding. I chose the latter as my mother was not in a financial position to do the former. I left school, moved away and worked as a live-in nanny. I was very lonely during those months, as I had no contact with friends. In their eyes it would be unforgivable, and I feared their rejection. I told my friends I had a job up north, and my mail was redirected to me so as not to arouse suspicion. This may sound extreme to you, but at the time it was better than living in my own community, completely ostracized. Thank God beliefs and values have changed drastically in the past two decades. Yet I am sure there are still quite a few people who would be horror-stricken that I did such a thing.

I only had one opportunity to see you. One evening I sneaked down the corridor, peered through the glass and saw the back of you sleeping peacefully. You had lots of dark hair. You have probably inherited a lot of your birth father's features. Anyway, since that day twenty-three years ago I have wondered what you look like.

You may be afraid to meet me. I know I am to meet you. It's like opening up a Pandora's box. Yet I am sure we share similar feelings and traits, like a void in our life or something not quite complete.

My biggest fear is that you may despise me for giving you up. I have always hoped and fantasized that you were placed in a good home with a lot of love and opportunities. I do hope your parents are aware that you have registered with the agency. I hope, if all goes well, that I will have an opportunity to meet them, as I have often wondered what they were like. Most of all I don't want them to have a lot of anxiety or fears about our meeting. I want our meeting to bring us closer to a lot of unresolved questions. Most of all I want to see what you look like and know that you are okay.

Maybe this December 14th I will be able to say, "Happy birthday, Susan," to you instead of saying it to myself.

10

Now I Can Explain

*I feel as if part of my heart has come
home again . . . and I am whole once
more.*

Micki Stocks

*T*HE REUNION *between an estranged birth parent and child
is always emotional, often "strange." For many mothers
there is an intense physical experience akin to the bonding
between mother and baby at the start of life. Sometimes it
resembles "love at first sight." Mothers describe their sense of
relief or release, of being whole again. But no one can predict
how events will unfold.*

*Rishy Powell's thoughts were mixed as her husband drove her
to her reunion with her birth son:*

My husband knew I was very nervous. I got out of the car and
he said, "I'll call you in an hour, and if the connection is good,
then we'll go out for lunch. I love you." I went up in the lift,
thinking, What am I doing here? He's not my kid! Why did you
get yourself into this mess in the first place? I decided to relax,
calm down and go in there, get it over with, take a look at him,
then I could leave. I walked into the office, past the social worker
and right into the room where Steve was standing. Our eyes met

and I said, "Oh, my God, you are mine, Steve! You are mine!" It was as if an explosion went off in my head. I saw my mother, my brother, myself — all my family — in him. I knew at that moment that this dark-skinned, brown-eyed man was my son. We hugged, we cried a little bit and we sat and talked. He didn't blame me for anything.

Afterwards he met my husband, and we went out for lunch. Steve fell in love with my husband right away and calls him Dad. My husband is very proud of him. Steve is an entrepreneur, has a family, a home, two cars and is doing very well. This is what my husband admires in a man, that he's able to do these things for himself. To me, sitting there with them in the restaurant, it was as if he'd found his father, not his mother. That's how I felt. When we would get together even after that, he was more into Dad than me. I was sort of on the sidelines. He'd talk business with my husband.

Once Pat Tyler was reunited with her son Paul, they had to re-establish the maternal bond that had been severed:

I pulled into the car park and saw this person I knew had to be him. He came up to the car, and I got out. Because I hadn't seen him since he was a baby, it was very strange. We hugged. I was a little bit nervous. He's a stranger; he's your son: it's a strange experience. We went to a restaurant, and I showed him some things. He started to cry, and I wondered why. I didn't cry until later.

We did a lot of hugging that first night and just holding each other. That was an experience I cannot adequately describe. It was almost like an electric charge — we were bonding. Once we'd done that it was as if all the other stuff didn't matter anymore. We were physically bonding. When a mother bonds with her child there is all that handling. My only regret is that we didn't do more of it that night. You feel awkward, but it was wonderful. I wish I had stayed longer and that we had lain down on his bed and just held each other.

After a two-hour phone conversation with her birth daughter, Debra Johnson was about to meet her at the shopping centre in Edmonton where she worked:

I had phoned my husband and told him the news. That night he asked me if I would like him to drive me to the meeting. I said, "No, no, I can do it." I drove over there, and all the time I was looking in the mirror, wondering how I looked. Tears were running down my cheeks. I was wiping away the tears, then looking again in the mirror. I got to the shopping centre, and my heart was absolutely racing. I could hardly breathe. I could hardly stand it at that point, I was so close. I thought, Should I walk past the shop and look in? I didn't know what to do. Then I thought, No, I'm just going to walk directly in, and I did.

There she was. I could have recognized her because she said she was tall and blonde, with blue eyes. She had her back to me, and all the fellows were standing around talking to her. I said, "Lori." She turned around, and of course, there were big hugs and kisses. It was unbelievable.

Micki Stocks says that just having her birth son's name, address and telephone number was incredible to her: "I loved to just look at it!" Soon afterwards she accompanied her husband to Toronto on a business trip so that she could meet David:

I could hardly believe that it was happening! I phoned David the moment we arrived to make arrangements to meet the next day. I remember writing in my diary: "I have waited forever for this! My son, my son, I can hardly wait to see you, to touch you, to see you smile and to hold you in my arms. And most of all to finally tell you to your face how very much I love you and have always loved you."

The next morning David met me at the hotel, and we spent the whole day together. It was very emotional. We were very much at ease with each other from the first moment — talking, laughing and looking at photographs. It was fun to discover how much alike we were in personality, likes and dislikes. I felt like I was living in a dream! The next evening he and I had supper at a lovely Italian restaurant and spent more time getting to know each other. I could hardly take my eyes off him! He was a handsome, intelligent, articulate young man, and he was my son! It still seemed like a miracle.

I look forward to my beloved son being part of the rest of my life. I know that he will always be part of his adoptive family. But now he will be a part of our lives, and I am truly grateful. I feel as if a part of my heart has come home again . . . and I am whole once more.

A reunion may turn back the clock, but it cannot change the past. Yet the opportunity to discuss the events that led up to the adoption allows a birth mother to purge herself of grief and guilt. When Mary-Jane Brodie finally met her daughter, Bonnie, it was in a restaurant. Time stood still as they soaked in the answers to eighteen years of curiosity:

Bonnie and I reached for each other at the same time and hugged and wept, and hugged and wept some more. We couldn't keep our eyes off each other, and needless to say, our pizza was untouched.

We chatted and exchanged gifts. She gave me pictures of her growing-up years that Bonnie and her mother had put together for me. The message written inside from Bonnie's mother was, "I hope you enjoy these pictures and hope you will add many more in the years ahead."

My gift to Bonnie was a gold chain and charm, exactly like the one I wore. The charm was the anchor, cross and heart which I always believed was a symbol of my faith and my love, and my hope of meeting my daughter someday.

I cried eighteen years' worth of relief when I went home on that special day.

Valerie Hamilton was a resident of Canada, while the daughter she had relinquished was living in England. Shocked and overjoyed that her daughter had at last found her, she could hardly wait for their reunion. Unfortunately her daughter was about to go on holiday for three weeks and asked Valerie to call when she returned:

For those three weeks I was absolutely dying. On the Monday morning of the day, I set my alarm for 2 am Canada time, 8 am British time, to make sure I got them when they got in. The following week my daughter was over here in Canada, and for me it's been fantastic. She's married to a lovely guy, and they're moving here to Canada.

She didn't get along too well with her adoptive family. It was, I think, a personality clash. They were totally different people from the background I came from. Her parents divorced when she was ten and she lived with her father, so she had always wanted a mother.

It's now coming up to six years since we found each other. She's back and forth and I'm back and forth and our phone bills are astronomical!

Margaret King needed to tell her son that she had never intended to give him up for adoption, but that because she had been only fifteen when she gave birth, the system had steamrollered her plans to bring him up. Now that he was an adult, she was thrilled with the prospect of meeting him. He wrote to his birth mother and

apologized for where he was — in prison. They had to wait until
he was released into a halfway house before they met:

My husband kept teasing me, asking if I wanted to turn back.
Not a chance! I will never forget those first moments with him.
This beautiful young man with long, flowing hair was my baby.
I wrapped my arms around him, and he wrapped his around me,
and I cried, laughed and cried some more. My heart was finally
whole again. The silken thread that had bound us all these years
had finally brought us together.

When Jean Clark phoned her daughter Debbie to arrange the first
meeting she found that her daughter preferred to meet somewhere
quiet:

She didn't want to go anywhere where there were other people.
I picked her up and that was really great, and she sat in the car
and said, "So how are you?" or "How have you been?" or
something like that.

I said, "Let me look at you for a while. I just want to look at
you."

That morning I had got a warning from my father. Debbie
had said she wanted to go to a park just to talk, and my father
had said to me, "Don't go anywhere where you could be
harmed." He was afraid that she might harm me. It's hard to
appreciate that there was so much negativity surrounding the
event at the time. I think the only thing that puts it together is
the reunion.

Those who search may find themselves frustrated by deadends and
endless bureaucracy. For this reason they seek outside agencies —
detectives who specialize in helping to find missing persons, or
counsellors.

Janet Turner and the birth father of her son sought counselling before they approached him and were advised to write to his adoptive parents, which, in this case, caused further upset:

Only the adoptive father wrote back to us and he said our son was "outraged." Then we were advised by the Post Adoption Centre to leave it until he was twenty-five. I couldn't. I became obsessed. That is the right word, and quite common I'm told.

I telephoned. I don't think I would have spoken if I thought our son had answered, but it was an older voice. He talked, and I wanted to keep him talking. My heart and head were pounding. I tried to say I didn't want to substitute, take away or in any way stop their love for each other. He said it must be hard to part with a child, but then switched and said that if I or my consort tried to contact or phone again, he wouldn't answer. He said, "Good day, madame," and put down the phone.

The most important thing, though, was that he told our son that I had phoned, which couldn't have been easy, I'm sure. Two weeks later we had a phone call from our son one Saturday night. When could we meet? I was so excited and his birth father, my partner, was, too. We were so nervous.

We met at a neutral place, as recommended by the Post Adoption Centre — a pub. It was a sunny day. We sat waiting for him to come in. I couldn't stop staring. I like him, I love him, I lust after him.

11

Guess Who's Coming
to Dinner?

*Things just weren't "everyday normal"
anymore.*

Wendy Appleby

*T*HE MAJOR PLAYERS *in any reunion may be the birth parent
and child, but they are not alone in being affected by it.
Reassembling the missing pieces of an adoptive triangle
can either threaten or enrich other family relationships. A
husband may resent the intrusion of his wife's birth child into
the existing domestic order. Siblings may have difficulty ad-
justing to a new family arrangement. On the other hand, an
only child may be thrilled to discover an older brother or
sister.*

*Because other family members and loved ones are often swept
into these new relationships, unforeseen problems can emerge,
as Pat Tyler was soon to find out:*

My other kids had to adjust. My son Steven had to lose his
number one spot. All of a sudden I'm the mother of a teenager
or young man, yet I hadn't grown up with him. I sometimes
wonder how to deal with it.

Her reunited son, Paul Patterson, also had many new relationships to adjust to:

I've got a fourteen-year-old half brother, an eight-year-old half sister and a couple of months ago I met another one of my birth father's irresponsibilities! I phoned her and asked, "Are you sitting down? This is your brother." She was totally open. She was raised as an only child and thought it was great that she had a big brother now.

Pat's children took to me immediately. My brother is into hockey, and I used to play, so we played hockey together. My little sister climbs all over me. It's amazing.

I just made contact with my birth father's mother, so I have to meet her. I've already met Pat's mother. Meeting these new family members has become easy now. It's no problem. I wasn't even nervous when I met my sister. You don't really get used to it, but you become an expert in the field, and you know how to deal with it properly.

Pat's mother felt odd about meeting me. Pat was living with her when she was pregnant, and she made the decision that she didn't want Pat to bring me home and to give me up for adoption. I'm sure this must be a major slap in her face, twenty-seven years later. She didn't know what to do; I could tell. It didn't matter to me. I hugged and kissed her. Every time we meet it seems to get better. She doesn't seem as uncomfortable as she did at the beginning; she's handling it pretty well. I'm sure a lot of things must be going through her mind. She's not going to get any sympathy from me but I understand.

Rishy Powell had waited so long to be reunited with Steve, yet time had passed and other people were now involved:

This was a fantasy that became a reality, and I was overlooking all the faults because I didn't want to see any; I had tunnel vision.

When reality started setting in I started seeing his faults, and he probably saw mine. I had a life before, but I didn't have a daughter-in-law or grandchildren. Are they going to infringe on my privacy? How am I going to manage this? Do I want this? Is it fair to my husband or other children? Now my children aren't in the spotlight, my grandchildren are. My oldest son is not my oldest anymore, and my youngest is not my youngest because I have grandchildren that are my babies. It affects everybody. When you start out to have a reunion you think it's just you and the child. It's not. It's a second family: grandparents, aunts and uncles, children, siblings, cousins. It involves so much more than you think it does.

It took a while, and then my children started telling me how they felt. My brothers are close to Steve and like him, but they really don't have a history with him. Whenever we get together as a family Steve is included. In a way, I'm lucky because Steve doesn't have a family. He left his adoptive parents' home when he was sixteen. His father isn't alive, and his mother's in her eighties and senile. So, he came here as my son. He says I'm the only mother he's ever had. I tell him that that's not right, that he should see his mother and he should allow her to see his children, because she is their grandmother. I don't care how she treated him, she still gave him a roof over his head. Anyway, there's only so much I can say before I start to sound like a nagging mother.

The adoptee may now have a family of his own. Rishy remembers that her son Steve did not tell his children that she was their grandmother until they had had an opportunity to get to know each other:

Alana came walking down the hall as if she had a mission. I knelt down, and she put her arms around me and said, "I know who you are." She held on to me, and I could feel her heart pounding and I couldn't let go. I was so uncomfortable, my leg was cramped, but I wouldn't let go until she was ready. That's when we bonded.

When the daughter Debra Johnson gave up for adoption finally contacted her, one of the first things she did was to tell her children the news she had kept from them for so many years:

When Barry, eight, came home, I took him into the bedroom and explained the story to him and said, "Do you understand what I said?"

He said, "Oh, yes." He must have understood fairly well because he went to school the next day and wrote this lovely story about how mother had this baby and kept it a secret for a long time and then finally broke the secret.

After the longest wait of his life, David Oxford was overjoyed to have found his birth daughter, Margaret. Now he has to deal with the other members of his family:

My wife has been very supportive throughout my search, and arrangements are going to be made for Margaret to meet her maternal grandparents, at their request, and also my mother. Eventually she will meet all of her extended family, including my daughter, Margaret's half sister.

It is one of my biggest regrets that I only told my daughter about her half sister after I had found Margaret. I should have told her years ago. I implore all your readers not to make the same mistake as I did. It is of great importance not to keep this kind of secret from the ones you love.

Wendy Appleby had known for years that her mother had given up her firstborn daughter for adoption. Although meeting her half sister Pam had brought out all kinds of conflicting feelings, their relationship is now a very successful one:

I felt very overwhelmed with mixed-up feelings, feelings that seemed to contradict each other. I was really excited and curious; this peaked when I learned her personality was much like mine and that she looked a lot like me. These similarities helped me relinquish any pessimism because I felt closer to her. On the other hand, I felt somewhat resentful that I was being compared to her. I didn't want someone to be just like me because I felt this meant I could be replaced.

It was especially hard considering the geography of the situation. Pam lives twenty minutes away from my aunt, uncle and cousin, near Windsor, Ontario. My maternal grandparents often visit there also. I felt that by living down in Nova Scotia I was losing out, as if I couldn't defend my position in my aunt's and grandparents' lives. I was envious of Pam's accessibility. I felt that my relatives would be closer to Pam now than to me. These thoughts seemed very childish to me (and they still do) yet they haunted me.

I also felt displaced. I was confused as to what my identity or position in the family would be now that Pam was a reality. Was I still the oldest child or grandchild? If not, what am I (especially since I am my dad's firstborn)?

In contradiction to my feeling of displacement, it was a novelty to know I have an older sister. It was something I always dreamed about. In that respect I was sad we hadn't grown up together and done those sisterly things.

Something that added a twist to my thoughts was the fact that Pam is married and has a seven-year-old girl. It was exciting to realize I was an aunt, but at the same time I felt something was taken away from me. It's really stupid, but it shattered the image of my being the one to have the first grandchild.

Other things that bogged me down at the time of initial contact were the reactions of my dad and grandparents. I was afraid they wouldn't be as happy or accepting as my mom was. I was concerned about their feelings and worried about being torn between them and my mom. My fears were put to rest right from the start. My dad arrived home while my mom was talking to Pam for the first time. I told him who she was talking to, and he immediately smiled. Without my dad's expression of support, I think it would have been especially hard for me. My grandparents have been quite receptive and made a special effort to contact me, since they were concerned about how I felt about the situation.

It was hard at first also because it seemed everywhere I turned there was talk about "Pam, Pam, Pam . . . " Mom was talking to Pam a lot and to relatives and friends about her. Things just weren't "everyday normal" anymore. Everything I said, heard and thought was about Pam. It was overwhelming! I'd try to plunge myself into something outside the house, but even my own head would rattle with "Pam" thoughts. It was crazy.

Even when Wendy finally met Pam, she says, "My emotions were like a rollercoaster — up and down, up and down." They spent a week together:

I was very sad to leave. It seemed stupid to end something that was only just beginning. Pam was crying nonstop. It was then I realized how important we were to her. I just melted and felt somewhat guilty for all my feelings of anxiety earlier. Pam gave me a really big, strong hug. I thought she'd never let go, but I didn't really want her to. It was comforting to know she felt affection towards me, just as I did for her.

I am very grateful Pam located us and is now actively a part of our family. Despite the perplexity of the experience, it was definitely well worth it. I have learned a lot about myself and my relationships. More importantly, I have gained some very special new relationships. I look forward to what the future brings us. Pam is the kind of person I'd want to know even if we weren't related. It makes me think of that saying I read somewhere: "Chance made us sisters, Hearts made us friends." A lifetime friendship is the best gift, I believe.

Edith Smith lived with the pain of giving up her daughter for twenty-five years. When a reunion was about to take place, she was overcome with emotion, yet still concerned about how her other family members would accept the news:

As for now it's exciting and too long in coming, yet coming too quickly. My father knows about her birth but not that she's searching. My husband knows about her and that I'd registered. We have three children, teenagers, who don't know and soon have to be told. It's a really frightening prospect to tell them. Are they going to be angry, excited, understanding, open to a meeting? How to tell them — one at a time or all together? That's really the only hurdle now.

Laurie Vitt says, "I sadly and reluctantly gave up my child twenty years ago." After experiencing a strong sense that her daughter needed her, she registered with the Children's Aid Society, without telling her husband, who was the birth father. When her daughter was ready for a reunion, however, Laurie did not receive the support from her husband she had hoped for:

I informed my husband what I had done, and he became very angry, as he felt she was a biological mistake and not our child, that if I wanted to pursue this I would be doing it on my own and that he didn't want to hear anything about it, even if it meant a divorce.

I still had to do it even if I had to face the consequences, as I felt a birth mother feels different from a birth father, and he couldn't and wouldn't understand. Needless to say, I made contact with my daughter a few weeks later.

On our anniversary, my husband came around. He gave me a

wonderful card and indicated that his daughter had a right to know who her father was. She came to see us, and we had a wonderful visit. I came to realize that biological factors are very prevalent, even if people grow up apart. She has a lot of my characteristics.

The reason I had the feeling that she needed me when she was fifteen years old was because she was going through a turmoil with her own parents and wanted to live with her natural parents. She knew we were young when she was born and thought we would understand her. Could it have been ESP?

Since the reunion she has had a baby out of wedlock. When I questioned my counsellor about it, she indicated that it's very common for adopted people to feel they don't belong and that this is the only way they really feel they have someone that belongs only to them.

Allison, my birth daughter and her real sister Cheryl have become very close. It took Cheryl some time to get used to the idea that she had a sister, as she'd always wanted one. Unfortunately, nine months later my husband and I separated. Allison has always felt that she contributed to the break-up, and to a certain point, she did. I had been unhappy for several years, and she made me realize that I now had something to change for.

Six weeks after Debbie Coward was born she was placed in the arms of an adoptive family and grew up as an only child. When she set out on a search for her birth mother, she found a whole new life.

I got married at eighteen to a local man I had been going out with since I was thirteen. For as long as I can remember I had wanted to trace my birth mother, but getting married seemed to make the need greater. After an extensive search of nearly four years I traced her, also my father, whom she had married just after I was adopted. We met, and I found that I had two younger sisters. After the usual difficulties we had a fairly good relationship. I became very close to my younger sister, who was very much like me. She spent a lot of time at my house and would go out with us wherever we went. Eighteen months ago my husband of seven years left me for my younger sister.

My story is not all despair as last October I met and fell in love with Simon, who is now living with me. I think the reason we get on so well is that he is also adopted.

Andy MacKay was in his mid-thirties when he found out his mother had given up an older brother, Bruce, for adoption. Bruce was living in Australia, and his obsession to find his birth mother was ruining his life. He finally tracked her down, however, in Canada.

After years of living with his obsessive compulsive behaviour, his wife could no longer deal with Bruce, and they separated. Bruce continued his search and was elated when Parent Finders called to say they had located his mother. It was too late though. The damage was done. Bruce's depression had become overbearing, and his psychiatrist had put him on medication to help alleviate some of the stress. My mother spoke to him twice and had received a few letters. She said he was beginning to get his life in order and that perhaps one day he and his wife would get back together. His quest was over — he had finally spoken to his mother and found out that he had brothers, three of them.

This is getting hard for me now. One evening, after being with friends, Bruce committed suicide. The pain I feel is real, and I think of my brother every day. I wish I could at least have talked to him. It's almost six years since Bruce died, but I feel like it was yesterday. I see a psychiatrist for other reasons, but Bruce is my main source of confusion now. I can't tell my mother about this because I know how much more pain it would cause. My problems are simple compared to what she must deal with each and every day.

The reunion between adoptee Jerry Appleton and his sisters resulted in instant bonding:

We became very, very close. We spent a lot of time together. One of them was closer in spirit to me — Lynn, the youngest — and, naturally, we gravitated to each other. We became absolute best friends. We shared things that we had never spoken out loud to ourselves. We would sit in front of the fireplace until six in the morning, talking about our past lives and our present lives. We became so very close that, when I found out the mistake, about six months later, I decided that I was the only one to know this mistake and that I would not tell anyone that I was not related to them.

I lived with it for five weeks, and then a dear friend of mine convinced me that in time I would be ridden with guilt, pull away from them and hurt them tremendously. He was right. I found the courage, got some deli food (which has always been part of my solutions to all problems in life) and a bottle of wine, borrowed a thirty-nine-foot yacht from a friend of mine and took Lynn sailing. I guess I was trying to set a better scenario, I don't know. I told her. We sat on that boat for the rest of the afternoon and cried. By the end of the afternoon, we had both come to the conclusion that the one thing we couldn't lose was the friendship we had nurtured. She almost convinced me that the rest of the family would feel the same way. I wasn't totally convinced; I was still frightened.

If it hadn't been for Lynn I wouldn't have had the courage, but, hand in hand, we told her sister and her mother, Jean. As it turns out, she knew. This is a beautiful twist, and the romantic fibre of the story that I love. Jean told me she had known about three or four weeks before. She had been shocked when I said I was born in 1941 because she suddenly realized, before I did, that we were talking about two different kids. It's created a bond between Jean and me.

Jean had decided to keep the same secret I had decided to keep because, when this story began, Lynn, who has multiple sclerosis, had difficulty walking. By the time we found out about the mistake, Lynn was in remission and walking without aid and doing extremely well. So her mother thought that all this love and laughter she'd shared with me had been the best medicine for her, and she was going to take the secret to her grave.

Lynn and I told the rest of the family, and every single one of them, without exception, greeted the news first with tears and, second, with a warm hug. My relationship with each one of them has deepened.

Three or four months later, Lynn and I discovered something that was quite shocking — that we were in love. It was not like falling in love because we were still living the transition; we were still, in some part, brother and sister, in spirit anyway. We shared it over a pizza. At that stage there was a young lady who was interested in a relationship, and I was hiding from it. Lynn was scolding me about it over this pizza, saying that I should take this seriously and follow it up. I kept saying, "No, I don't want to deal with this." Finally, pressured, I said, "I can't do that because I'm already in love." She thought I was putting her off and insisted I give her a name. Finally I said, "Her name is Lynn."

She started to cry. At that moment the waiter came to the table and was a little baffled by the tears. He didn't know what to say and said, "Is everybody okay?"

She looked at him and said, "I love broccoli," because there was broccoli on the pizza we had. That was it. Lynn and I are planning on getting married in May of next year.

And what role is the birth parent expected to play in a family that has suddenly grown overnight? Rishy Powell soon found out:

I had to become a mother, a mother-in-law and a grandmother all at once, and that was very hard. I couldn't get to the grandchildren until I got through Steve, then my daughter-in-law.

Steve and my other boys all seemed to fit together. They all got along so well. It was as if Steve had been away on a long, long holiday and had just come back. Everything was beautiful.

However, after the elation of her reunion, Rishy Powell had to tell the world that she had found her long-lost son:

I had to tell everybody about him. That was the hardest thing for me. My cousins couldn't believe it because we were a very close family. They were all there to support me. Even my in-laws were ecstatic for me, because I think everybody has a skeleton in their closet. Everybody was very supportive and very, very happy for me. This was good for me, but it was very hard to tell them. Can you imagine if those people hadn't supported me? I probably would have shot myself.

12

Remember Us?

*Does anyone think of us and what our
feelings might be?*
John and Lynda Hansen

*I*N THE MIDST *of all this excitement, from one side of the triangle, the adoptive parents look on. These are the people who nursed the child when sick, rocked him to sleep, helped him get ready for school each day and steered him through the many pitfalls of growing up. Will the reunion between their child and his birth parent threaten their family unit? Will their child now cleave to another?*

John and Lynda Hansen believe the media forgets the dedicated role played by most adoptive parents and their involvement in many reunions:

What is usually overlooked in all the stories is the fact that adoptions are a triangle — adoptee, birth parents and adoptive parents. When reunions do occur, all the attention is focussed on the adoptee and the birth parent. The feelings of the adoptive parents are often overlooked, not even considered.

We are adoptive parents of two children (now adults) and are involved in one reunion. Now that the reunion has taken place, we have mixed feelings regarding the reunion and still hope that the end result will be emotionally satisfying to all in our triangle.

On our son's twentieth birthday we noticed an advertisement in the personal column from a birth mother wishing to make contact with a child she put up for adoption. The place of birth and the date coincided with our son's birth. We contacted the Triad Society to see if this was our son's birth mother. It was indeed our son's birth mother, and her concern was for his welfare. Was he still alive? Was he well? Through the society, we assured her that all was well and sent a picture and advised her that when we thought the time was right, we would get our son to contact her. We still remained anonymous, as we wanted to go at a slow pace so it wouldn't be a sudden shock to our son, even though he has known since he was a small child that he was adopted.

On his twenty-first birthday a similar advertisement appeared in the paper, and we decided that now was the time to tell him his birth mother was looking for him. Ironically, one of his fellow workers also saw the advertisement and showed it to him. When he came home from work we told him about it, and he said, "I've already seen it, but didn't know how to tell you. I didn't want to upset you."

Our son sat on it for quite some time and finally decided to write her a note. Thus contact was made and subsequently they met. The birth mother lives out of town and has made several trips to visit our son. On each occasion she was invited to have coffee or lunch with us, and she always declined. At her request they met in neutral territory and would go on from there. Our son has been to her home, has met her family and has appeared to have had a good time. However, she is still not prepared to meet us: thus our mixed feelings.

After raising, caring for and loving our son, and seeing him through all the chickenpox, measles, tonsils, etc., the third party in our triangle appears to ignore the role that we have played for the past twenty-two years. From this situation, here are some of the questions that run through our minds:

Does anyone think of us and what our feelings might be?

Does anyone know how threatened we can feel by this other person?

Does anyone know how it can hurt knowing she can do no wrong in our son's eyes?

Why do people refer to the birth parents as the "real" mother or father? Does that make the adoptive parents "fake" parents?

As you can see, we do not feel that our son's birth mother considers how we feel. It's like dealing with a shadow. We were the ones who allowed her the privilege of knowing him and considered her feelings.

We would be very reluctant to go through this again with our other child, now that we know the hurt that can be caused when the triangle is broken. We keep these thoughts to ourselves, as we know it bothers our son, and we hope that one day this estrangement will be overcome and we will "all live happily ever after."

Jeff and Pamela Barnett, the parents of two adopted children, give us a further insight into their side of the triangle. Although one of the adoptions is open, even today this is not a common occurrence:

The attitude of society towards adoptive parents is that we don't exist. There have been many articles in newspapers and magazines on the subject of adopted children seeking their roots. Yet there is little, if any, consideration given to the feelings of adoptive parents who have nurtured and raised their children for many years. Society seems to be hung up on "biology." Not only does the adoption process have little concern for the feelings of adoptive parents, society feels that there is something terribly wrong with a woman if she cannot produce a child by biological means.

We have a story to tell. We are the proud parents of two adopted children. Our four-year-old daughter has all the information about her birth mom available to her at any time. In fact her birth mom has seen her on a number of occasions. She is adopted herself and understands the whole process. Our three-month-old son will have almost no information, as his mom would prefer to forget she was ever pregnant, let alone gave birth to a beautiful son. In both adoptions we had absolutely no choice in terms of how we would like to be involved with the birth mother or the postnatal care. It was fully the mother's decision.

In the case of our daughter, the biological mother and grandfather were truly wonderful. They showed a great deal of concern for us and our feelings by allowing us to be present at her birth. They asked that we assume her postnatal care. If it had been up to the hospital and the social workers, we would have had to wait at home for fourteen days, not knowing if the birth mother would change her mind or not.

We have cared for our son since the day he left hospital, but as he is only three months old, we are still not totally "out of the woods." His mother can still change her mind, irrespective of the fact that we have assumed total care and that she never saw him in the hospital.

It has been a particularly long road for us, as Pam has endured many surgeries and two failed attempts at *in vitro* fertilization. But in some respects that is not half as bad as how some people have treated us. Many times people have cruelly asked Pam why she hasn't produced any children. She has also endured numerous parties and outings where other women have gone on about the trials and tribulations of their pregnancies and birth experiences.

We feel rather hurt that all the recent attention towards adoption reunions serves to belittle the role of adoptive parents, as if we were second-class citizens. For us this is epitomized in a statement a social worker made to us at a mandatory adoption meeting. She was a woman in her early thirties who told a room full of infertile parents that we could never love an adopted child as much as we would love our own biological one.

We feel it is important that society becomes more sensitive to the third side of the triangle.

It is true. There are millions of adoptive parents who are not news. What is noteworthy about a mother walking her child to school? What is remarkable about comforting a sick child? What is special about reading a bedtime story? This is the role of every parent. What does become news is when a birth parent is reunited with her child.

Antonia Benjaminsen, the adoptive parent of two sons, feels the discrimination keenly:

How do you explain that you are always the ones left out of the stories of reunion, always play the role of the Good Sports or the substitutes who perhaps wanted, but were unable, to fill the needs of their child? These children were received and raised in love, were often much more cherished than some people's natural offspring are.

As the adoptive parents of three girls, Grace King feels left out of the reunion equation. She says that when the adoptions were made, she and her husband were assured that there would be complete confidentiality and that the children's birth parents would never find them:

Our two older daughters have found their birth parents, and the youngest is searching. I feel something has gone out of our relationships.

These birth parents have other children and will have grandchildren by them. We have only our adoptive children and grandchildren to share.

Jean Clark was advised to visit a counsellor and found it helped her to empathize with the pain the adoptive parents felt after her reunion with her daughter:

It helped me to understand the adoptive mother, helped me to relate to what she was feeling. Now we talk on the phone regularly, usually for about two hours, just getting to know each other.

Jane Reeves had a reunion with her birth mother that left her "totally overwhelmed," and she had assumed they would enjoy a close relationship in the future:

I was advised by the agency that my adoptive parents should be told about my finding my birth mother. I didn't agree. I felt sure they wouldn't understand my need to find her. As far as they were concerned I was their daughter. I gave the matter considerable thought, and finally some weeks later I told them. Oh, I wish I never had!

They were really upset and hurt. They didn't understand and made me promise never again to see this woman who had given me away. It seemed the easiest thing to do at the time. They were so hurt; my father even cried.

I tried to make my birth mother understand, but it was very hard. I haven't seen her since. Nine years have now passed, but we keep in touch by the odd letter or phone call. However, given an ultimatum — her or them — what choice could I really have made?

The relationship with my parents has never been fully restored. They never mention the matter at all, but I know they have never really forgiven me. I wish there had been a book I could have read about other people's experiences before I went ahead. Oh, don't get me wrong, I don't regret my decision to find my birth mother, but I wish I had understood more about my parents' reaction.

Following his successful reunion with his birth mother, the time came for Paul Patterson's adoptive parents to meet the mother who had borne him:

I was really hesitant in telling them because when you tell most people that you've met your birth parents they say, "Oh, but what about your adoptive parents?" What about them? I love them, but people say I'm hurting their feelings. In my mind that's garbage. My adoptive parents had open minds about it, but that's not that normal. A lot of adoptive parents feel really threatened. I can see it if you're eight years old, but I'm twenty-seven and not living at home anymore. They're not losing anything.

I told them over the phone that I'd met Pat. It wasn't easy. They both cried, but both said, "That's great! You should have done it earlier, and we would have helped you." If I had known that maybe I would have. They thought it was a really good thing for me to do. My adoptive mother said something that really stuck in my mind, that there was enough love for everyone.

Pat was just dying to meet them. It would fill a void for her. A couple of weeks went by, and I phoned them again and talked to them about it. They said, "Great. Bring her over." So we went over there, and it was a very interesting experience for me. I was sitting on one side of the room, and over there were both my mothers. I tried to make light of the situation by saying, "Mother," and seeing two heads turn! It was a very good meeting, and they sent each other a couple of letters. I was at home recently, and I've never gotten along with them as well as I am now. It's great.

However, for David Fraser, an adoptive father, his daughter's search for her birth father has brought a great deal of anguish. Despite feeling that he had been a good father to her through her formative years, he says he has "been cast aside" for his daughter's birth father:

Even though she had my last name, even though she called me Dad and even though everyone said I was an excellent parent, Stephanie began rejecting me when she reached the age of eighteen and was allowed to make contact with her birth father.

The rejection started with her high-school graduation, to which she invited her birth father instead of me. Graduation is an official event in her life, and I'm her official father. How could she be so insensitive? What made finding this out even more painful was the fact that that afternoon I had picked up my new will, which made her the sole beneficiary of my estate.

The rejection continued over four years, particularly on Father's Day. People would ask me if I had received a card from my daughter, to which I would answer, "Oh, yes, Stephanie always chooses such a nice verse." But there was never a card. Nor was there a card on birthdays or at Christmas. The rejection was like having a knife plunged into my heart and twisted.

The straw that broke the camel's back was her wedding three years ago. Not only did she not ask me to give her away (she chose her grandfather instead), she didn't even invite me. We've been estranged ever since. Now I understand she's given birth to a child, my grandchild by law. I'll probably never see the boy or girl (I still don't know what it is).

What do I think of all this? I think my daughter is an ingrate, given all the loving sacrifices I've made for her. I also think she's cruel. I don't have the best father in the world, but I would never have let a Father's Day go by without giving him a card. It would have hurt him.

My advice to people considering adoption is to think twice. If there's a chance that the birth parent is going to show up in the future, you may be greatly disappointed.

It is easy to understand the negative feelings of many adoptive parents regarding reunions, but to stand in the way of a search can cause alienation within the family. Barbara Joan Hewett has been searching for her birth family for six years, to no avail. Her largest stumbling block is her adoptive mother:

I only wish I could find some little opening in this very large mystery. Because of my adoptive mother, I seem to be running into brick walls. She won't tell me anything, but I know she knows. Her reason for not telling me is that she is afraid I won't love her anymore. Little does she realize that it is only causing us to drift farther apart.

What is needed is an open relationship. It is, after all, the most healthy approach for all families, whether or not adoption is a factor. Although it may be difficult for the adoptive parent, some support their children in seeking out their roots. Nancy Graham and her husband adopted two children, and they have offered positive encouragement:

I think that because I had a cousin who was adopted and her mother would never discuss anything with her, it perhaps made me more open with our two children. Friends have questioned whether we really love our kids. Our reply is that of course we love our kids, but because of this love we feel they should be encouraged in everything, even in finding their roots.

Elsie Seward and her husband had told their son Craig as early as he could understand the concept that he was adopted. He grew up with a natural curiosity abut his roots, as well as suffering a sense of abandonment. In order to help him resolve his feelings, Elsie and her husband located Craig's birth mother:

He always told us that we would never stop being his parents if he found her.

As adoptive parents we have always felt, and still do, that every adopted child has a right to know their roots. When you think of the family network on both sides, it is hard to deny them their heritage.

Maureen Dinner's adoptive parents were very excited for her when she was about to meet her birth mother. They understood that this was something Maureen had to do:

My relationship with my adoptive parents didn't change through all this. They were very supportive of me the whole way, and I can't say I feel any different towards them than I did before. I remember thinking after that first meeting with my birth mother how convinced I was that we are a product of our environment and not of our genes. I am much more like my adoptive parents than my birth mother.

Nancy Verrier, an adoptive mother speaking at the 1992 conference of the American Adoption Congress, spoke on behalf of others in her position:

The issue of search sometimes makes many adoptive mothers wonder if the struggle was worth it. They often feel left out of the reunion experience, except to be considered a hindrance to that process. Although in my opinion they have no right to interfere in those searches and in fact should help, they too have a right to their feelings and they need to be heard.

It is important that each of the parties in any reunion understand each other's feelings. Although it is impossible to know what a birth mother handing over her child feels, or adoptees feel as they grow up, it is equally impossible to know how an adoptive parent feels. The successful ending to a search, they know, will change the relationship they have with their child in what way? It is easy for the adoptive mother to feel that the sudden appearance on the scene of the birth mother is a little late. After all, the work is finished. The child is now grown into a healthy adult. It's the last act, and here comes a figure from the wings to take the bows and bouquets. Why should she feel happy?

Diana Lintott, who, since her own successful reunion, helps others with their searches, comments:

A search for birth parents can create problems for adoptive parents. Some adoptees don't tell their parents of their search. In past years many adoptive couples were assured their children would never be able to trace their birth parents. The adoptive parents may fear they will be rejected if the "real" parents are located. Thankfully, this happens rarely, if ever. In all the reunions I'm aware of, it's never happened. One person said, "If a parent can love more than one child, surely a child can love two sets of parents." My own mother said that if she had been adopted, she'd want to find her roots, and encouraged me in my search.

Stephanie Lennox, an adoptee, addresses the chief concern of many adoptive parents when their children seek out their birth parents:

One reason I waited so long to begin my search was because of the respect I had for my adoptive mother. She had a great fear that if I ever did a search and found my birth parents I wouldn't love her anymore. My mother's fears were so strong that I never knew, or was told, very much. It is sad that my mother couldn't trust my judgement and have faith in me to be able to make decisions for myself.

I strongly believe that all people who want to adopt someone's child should always get as much information as possible from the agency about their adoptive child. They should also be completely prepared for the day that this child will ask, "Where is my real mother? Why did she leave me? Didn't she love me?" The children are going to ask those questions, and they need honest parents with honest answers. They will usually not love you less. They just have a need to know who they are and where they come from. Is that really so bad?

Alexis Roberts understands the concerns of the adoptive parent, while longing to have a relationship with the son she gave up for adoption:

It must be very painful for adoptive parents to worry about someone like me. I will never have what they had. I would like adoptive parents not to fear me. I can't take away the past twenty-three years; I simply want to share the remaining years in some way. Is that so bad or unrealistic?

I hear so many adoptive parents say that it is wrong that biological parents are allowed to come back into the picture. All I can say is that no one worried about me when I was that seventeen-year-old frightened teenager, when they literally took my son away from me. I've paid my dues, thank you. Face reality. I am not dead. I have a face. I am here. I am his biological mother, and nothing, absolutely nothing on the face of this earth can change that.

People must realize that the birth mother, the child and the adoptive parents are all connected. We are indeed a triangle. Without me there would be no child. Without the child there would be no adoptive parents. We're connected whether we like it or not.

Pamela Wruck later married the father of the son she put up for adoption and now regrets the decision to give up her child. She knows, however, that his loyalty is primarily with the parents who raised him:

Our birth son's connection to us is by blood. He is our natural birth son, and we are his natural, biological parents, but we are not his mother and father. His mother and father are the two people who loved, nurtured and raised him since infancy, regardless of the difference in lifestyles between us. Nothing can change the fact that he will never call us Mom or Dad.

Carol and Russ Gustavson, founders of the American organization Adoptive Parents for Open Records, have four adopted children of their own. They believe in renewing the connections with original families:

Life doesn't begin when a child is placed in your arms through adoption. They are born into original families. If we're going to teach our children to be truthful in life, they have to have the truth of their own heritage. You must be very secure in your relationships with your adopted children; many adoptive families feel that searching for birth parents is just opening up a can of worms. It makes me very angry when people decide what's best for somebody else. Our children didn't feel they were opening a can of worms; they were opening up the truth to their own lives.

Michael Blugerman recognizes the fact that during their adopted child's adolescence, often a stormy time in any family, adoptive parents may feel an added strain:

Frankly, most parents of biological children feel the same way. The children start going in their own direction, they're ungrateful and they're not listening to our advice and so on. But when you are adoptive parents, you have this added flavour: "Oh dear, this kid is really someone else's." You feel you're on borrowed time. I talk to a lot of adoptive parents and explain that the child may want information at a later date and that they should help them.

Some say, "Oh, I'm going to raise this child in such a wonderful way that he's not going to look for his parents." Which is a real shame because they put themselves in a trap. They then have to perform and do a good job or they're going to lose the child. And that's not the point at all. Some children want to look and some don't. It doesn't mean that the parents did a bad job or a good job. Some are just curious about their history, some couldn't care less.

The fact is, it's really a myth that we have all these successful reunions. It's true that there are a lot more reunions than ever before, but there are very few stories in which adoptees actually go off and create a relationship with their birth parents. It's really a small percentage. But because a reunion is such a dramatic story a lot of adoptive parents feel it's like that every time.

Clara and Leslie Will's adopted daughter Kirsten seemed to have little or no interest in who her birth parents were or where she could find them:

As she grew she never voiced a need to find her birth parents. But I have it ingrained in me that it's every child's right; I've always believed that if the adopted person wants to be reunited and the other party wants the same, then that is something they should be assisted with.

We had a law that almost came in in Ontario that would have denied the opportunity for children to find their birth parents. I was so angry I wrote letters and kicked up a hell of a stink. Anyway, when it was defeated I told my daughter, and all she said was, "Oh, that's good, Mom," and then went on with what she was doing.

She went through her life not thinking too much about her birth parents, and when she was a teenager she was caught up in her own life. So as she got closer to eighteen, I said to her, "You know, if you want to, you can register to find your birth parents." She agreed it was a good thing, and that was that. She never mentioned it again. Then as time went on I brought it up again. I must confess, I thought that if she ever did it it would take a long time. Anyway, when the time came, I said, "Do you want me to do this for you or not?" Then she said, "Yeah, that'll be a good idea." So I got the forms, she filled them out and I sent them in. Nobody thought about it, then some months went by, and I thought I'd just ring and find out. They said they had a backlog, and I thought, well, this is going to take about fifteen years. So we carried on with our lives. One day last summer a card arrived from the post office saying that there was a registered letter waiting for her to pick up. That day I was in a meeting in my office when I got a phone call from Kirsten, saying, "You know that registered letter I go? Guess what it was. My birth mother has registered too."

A shiver went down my spine. I said, "Are you excited?" She was as calm as could be.

Anyway, she was contacted by a counsellor, and another counsellor talked to the birth mother. They were very careful to make sure that they both wanted the meeting to take place.

A few days later another registered letter came, and Kirsten called me again. This time she said, "Guess what? My birth father has registered." As it turned out her birth mother and birth father had married after Kirsten had been born. They had registered on the same day.

So then we started to have exchanges of pictures and information back and forth between the counsellors. It got to the time when they asked Kirsten whether she would like to meet. They picked the lobby of a nice hotel, and she went down there and they met. It has turned out wonderfully. They really like each other.

I've now met and had lunch with her birth parents a few times. They come to our house to pick her up, and we really like them. The thing that's so interesting is that there's a lot about Kirsten that people have assumed she has learned from me, and yet now we've found her birth mother, we've discovered they have similar characteristics. Just little things, different ways about her.

I'd just like to say that as far as Kirsten is concerned, we are her real parents and they are her birth parents. That will never, never change. We're so close and we mean so much to each other that her getting to know her birth mother, even her coming to love her birth mother, has in no way ever given us a feeling of being threatened or a feeling that we'll lose her. Not at all.

13

A New Life Begins

*In finding my birth mother I really
found myself . . . and I liked what I
found.*

Sharon L. Schwede

ONCE THE REUNION *has passed and the excitement has died
down, what then? There is no established pattern for the
continuing relationship between birth parents and their
offspring. For some the path is smooth, but some find it rocky
and others decide to travel no further.*

*A reunion can trigger strong, sometimes primitive feelings.
Primary among these can be a sexual attraction between birth
parent and child, which can cause guilt and confusion. For the
birth mother, genetic sexual attraction is a manifestation of the
sensual experiences between mother and baby that she was
denied. She was not there to touch and stroke her infant. Is it
now too late? Rishy Powell broaches this subject, considered
taboo by many birth parents and their children:*

A while after Steve and I were reunited I started to have sexual
feelings. I couldn't understand why I was feeling this way towards my son! I raised three boys and never felt that way
towards them. I usually tell my husband everything, but I was

so ashamed of the way I was feeling that I couldn't bring myself
to tell him this.

I was talking to the social worker, and we were chatting
about how things were going after the reunion. We were just
about to end when she said, "Is that all you have to say?" I
said yes. She said, "Are you sure there's nothing else?" I said
no. She said, "Are you having any sexual feelings towards your
son?" I said, "What?" and she repeated it. I asked her why
she'd asked that, and she said it was because it's a very normal
thing.

I told her I couldn't believe I was feeling this way. She said
that it's not the sexual act you want, but that when you have a
baby you bathe it, you hold and kiss it — it's all sensual. I never
got to do that with Steve, and that's why I was feeling like this.
It was the touching of skin and holding each other that I wanted.
She said that there are many birth siblings who fall in love with
each other, mothers and daughters who strip themselves naked
and get into bed with each other just to feel their bodies, and
some women who even leave their husbands to live with their
sons. It's all part of missing the raising of your child. She sent
me some information on this and let me know that these feelings
were okay. Once she explained it to me, I never felt that way
about Steven again.

*Barbara Gonyo, who found her birth son, has led a support group
for thirteen years. She, like Rishy Powell, found herself attracted
to her son in a way that she had not experienced with her other
son. On forming her group she found that the term used for these
feelings was causing problems:*

The term "genetic sexual attraction" is one that sometimes
irritates people who say it's not really genetic, it's not really
sexual and it's not really an attraction. All of that may be true;
I don't know. When I came into the movement they were already

using that term, even though I've been credited with coining it because I'm the only one who ever seems to talk about it. I got the credit and the blame!

My feeling about genetic sexual attraction is that it is different from incest because you're dealing with people who have been separated for years and didn't get to know each other until they were brought back together in a reunion. It could be a mother and son, as in my own case, or a father and a daughter, or siblings.

The feelings are not fun when you have them. It's frightening to have sexual feelings for someone you're related to. It's a terrible feeling; it's really uncomfortable to be in a room with your relative and know that the only thing you can think about is going to bed. You don't think about anything else. You act like an idiot.

In my own case I acted like a sixteen-year-old girl every time he was in my presence. It made him totally uncomfortable, and it made me feel like a fool. And it wasn't anything I could seem to stop, so it made our relationship very frightening for him and kept him away from me more than it brought him to me. If I tried to ask him about his feelings, he wouldn't deny having them. He wouldn't say yes or no; he wouldn't say anything, which is how he deals with most things. So I just had to assume he was having them and wasn't able to talk about it. Because I was so fascinated by the subject and feeling these feelings, I started giving workshops, hoping more and more people would come to them.

Siblings have the strongest problem with this because they don't have the boundaries, haven't grown up together with the incest taboo. Brothers and sisters who are separated and then get back together can fall in love, without these boundaries. Getting them to have boundaries is what we need to be able to tell them about first. That's why in a support group it's important, in the initial phone call, that I tell them about genetic sexual attraction. I would rather they were forewarned that it's a possibility. I don't say it's going to happen to you, but it could happen to you.

It doesn't only happen with opposite-sex people either. It happens with same-sex people, too, because the bonding is very, very strong.

I was at a group meeting once, and my son walked into the room late. I looked up and had the weirdest feeling when he walked in the door. I didn't think, Oh, there's my son; I thought, That's me in the male form standing there. That was really crazy. There is that strong bond there, you feel that the person is so much a part of you. You're falling in love with them, and the part you're falling in love with is usually the part you like about yourself.

My main theory about genetic sexual attraction is that it is a strong need for intimacy — total intimacy. You can't be their mother, and they don't allow you to be their mother; you are to be their friend. That puts you in a peer position, where you're equal. If you're equal you can't get the mother/son thing, you can't get that kind of bonding, so you go for utter, total intimacy. And what is intimacy when you're an adult?

It was as if his father had come back into my life, an unfinished romance. He looks like him; he walks like him; he talks like him. So, what happened when my son walked into the room? I became sixteen.

I know reunited brothers and sisters who are living together as man and wife. I also know of a couple who even got married and live together. In their state they're allowed to marry because on paper they're not blood relatives. Most of these couples are still together after several years and very happy with each other, all thinking that nobody else knows, but I wonder what it will do to their families.

I know mothers and sons who have slept together, but usually that ends. I haven't heard of any fathers and daughters who have slept together, but I've heard a lot of men want to, they just won't talk about it.

Siblings are the biggest problem, I think, because they really do want to be married. Because they are peers, they do want to go out, get married, have families.

One case that came across our telephone wires was really interesting. It was a brother and sister who were both adopted into different families, then reunited, and were very attracted to each other. They decided to see their grandmother, whom neither of them had met before. She lived on a farm and welcomed them out there. Sometimes I think the grandmother was a little slow, but sometimes I think she was very clever. She couldn't get it into her head that these were adults and kept treating them like children. She supervised play for them; she had them playing as if they were little kids. But it was so effective that after a week they walked away feeling as if they could put their genetic sexual attraction behind them and be brother and sister, because they had experienced a week of childhood together. I don't think their grandmother did it consciously.

One of the things you can do for siblings who are experiencing genetic sexual attraction is to get them to play together. Maybe do some sand-tray stuff together, do some pictures together or play games together. Or, if it's a mother and son, let him sit on her lap. Let the brother and sister pull each other's hair. When we raise children we put them in the bath together, and they look at each other and don't know an elbow from a penis; it doesn't make any difference to them, it's all just parts. We can't do that when they're adults, but we can put some restrictions on them. Maybe put them in a swimming pool together so they're scantily clothed but not naked, so they can touch each other.

One woman talked about taking her son to a swimming pool. They were on holiday together. She'd always wanted to carry him, but he's a man now. When they were in the water she could do that, so she lifted him in the water and carried him across the pool, and they did some water play. She said it was wonderful and that's how they got some of these frustrations out — they did do something about it, but through "proper" behaviour.

This is something we need to help people through. It's part of the reunion process that is important.

Another thing I always tell those about to have a reunion is, "Don't set yourself up in romantic settings. Try a trip to the zoo instead."

I was in a workshop where a birth mother said she had met her daughter and they were so crazy about each other that she had her come and stay the night after they'd known each other a couple of months. They undressed, went to bed and slept together like spoons. She said it was wonderful and that there was nothing sexual about it.

Think about birthing today, where the baby is thrown on your stomach, chest or breast, and how wonderful that is. You're touching your child, skin to skin, for the first time — you're getting the smells, the baby is getting used to you, you're getting used to them. We didn't get that. Now what happens when, twenty-six years later, you want to go skin to skin and you want the baby on top of you? It's no different except that he's a lot bigger.

We feel it's so unnatural when we realize we're having sexual feelings for this person. I really did have sexual feelings for my son, and when I got them I would have loved to have been in bed with him. It was more than just bonding. It started out that way, but I wanted everything. He was the one who had the brakes and didn't have the feelings, so I was very lucky that we weren't sharing those feelings. I had to go through all that hell by myself. I look at my other son, and I don't feel any attraction for him. I raised him.

We gave up our children because of a sexual experience we weren't supposed to have. It was a thing we weren't supposed to do and we did, so we were bad. Now we find these kids, and again, it's to do with sex. Maybe it's all connected somehow.

Janet Turner's relationship with her birth son has had a year to develop, and she admits that genetic sexual attraction is a part of it:

What can I say? Words are inadequate. I still need counselling (he doesn't want counselling). Yes, it's true, sexual problems do exist, as recognized by some in adoption work. I do find him attractive, and I think he feels the same for me. We've not talked about it other than my telling him not to worry about the attraction.

We cuddle, kiss, and he has sucked my breasts. For me, this is not sexual love but a longing to fulfil a desire. I think it's been the same for him. My partner, the birth father, knows and is very understanding about it so far. It is frightening that I recognize a flare of my nostrils and am feeling something I'm not at present getting from my partner, which is an awful thing to admit. Am I punishing him?

I am aware that this reunion could be a threat to my relationship with my partner. I hope not and that we can work through it. I want to remain in contact with our son for the rest of our lives.

His adoptive mother told him that he has "betrayed" them by seeing us. He has come for three or four days at a time at weekends. So he is pulled in two directions. We are from quite different backgrounds. They are wealthy, and we are not. There are many physical likenesses between me and our son, and we have some similar habits. So much for nurture-nature theory. I see myself in him more than his birth father.

I am healthier in all aspects since I've found him. It's killed the ghosts, and I'm happier. It's harder now for him, but we hope it will work out.

*Naturally it is the aim of any search to lay to rest the ghosts of the
past. But successful or not, reuniting of adoptees and birth parents
can result in many other sources of unforeseen stress, too.*

*Jamie Boswell has been able to redirect the anguish of his
personal search into forming a support group to help others in
the adoption triad:*

My adoptive parents are very supportive. My older brother was
a heroin addict, and they thought by our searching we could find
some peace of mind. I was adopted into a very well-to-do, very
good family. I guess adoptive parents get a bad name, but these
were nice, nice people. They weren't abusive, they weren't
alcoholics, they were just great people, yet three out of the four
of us went bad for a while, and they really had a hard time
understanding what was going on. My mother said to me, "I just
never knew. Once I took you home I thought you were mine. I
didn't expect, twenty-six years later, that I'd be going through
so much pain." You get support, and then she gets very tired of
the whole thing — it goes back and forth. The only thing she
asks of us, which I didn't think was a big thing, was that we call
her "Mom" and we call our birth mothers by their first names.

I got involved with a group called Healing Adoptees, which
was using the twelve-step method as a tool to healing. Alcoholics
Anonymous, Co-Dependency, Self Parenting, Al-Anon, Ala-
teen — we took as many different twelve-step groups as we
could find, took a look at them and saw what they were trying
to do at each step. Then we changed it around. When I got into
it there were just four people, and then all of a sudden some
adoptive parents and some social workers wanted to come. Our
program wasn't set up, so I rewrote the steps, and we wrote a
lot of literature to involve everyone. We changed the name from
Healing Adoptees to Healing Adoption. I think people are
realizing you can go to monthly meetings as much as you want,
but it's just not enough. This is an organized path.

We use the steps as thought-provoking discussion topics and also as aids to healing, like admitting we are powerless over our pasts and over our adoption experiences. More birth mothers have a hard time admitting this, because they've been carrying the guilt and thinking, Oh, I could have done something. We just say you do the best you can with the tools you have.

This is a spiritual guide, so it has a lot of references to the higher power and asking your higher power to give you guidance. People are finding that it works. We've got about sixty people now, in three groups. The steps are just a tool; the fellowship is a big thing. There is guidance, acceptance, love — a lot of things like that. We stress feelings. It seems to be working well.

On the surface, Jane Thomas's reunion with her daughter a year ago seemed perfect. However, just below the surface lurked a personal crisis:

In my view, adoptees can claim success when they can confront their fantasies and fears, know their past, however painful, sad or depressing, and delight in finding a supportive new family and relations.

The reunion is very different for the birth parent. Often the denial of the initial acute loss is carried silently and secretly with no opportunity to feel the anger, the pain or the grief. Society attaches great shame to this, and the grief is socially unacknowledged. The shame, and the denied grieving process, is devastating and is carried throughout their lives. Like the adoptee who secretly experiences feelings like, Was I really born?, the birth mother asks, Did I really give birth?

When a reunion occurs, even if long sought and hoped for, it reopens all the unhealed wounds that surrounded the initial events. The effects on the parent of a reunion (which is usually unexpected) are extremely traumatic. This pain and regression cannot be shared with the newly discovered child because it has nothing to do with them. The birth parent fears the child may feel rejected and responsible if they become aware of the pain and grief stirred up by the reunion. It involves one's own unfinished business, the pain and trauma of the parent's own youth.

My reunion was truly joyful and happy for me, but the hidden agenda that followed was to heal myself within. I cried continuously for three months for the profound pain and grief I had been holding in for twenty-six years.

Also a major identity crisis takes place: Who am I? What is my role? The settling-in period takes a long time and must be approached gently and patiently. The question of identity and placement affects more than just the adoptee and birth parent. My daughter's adoptive mother and I have been a great support for each other.

Through my own recovery I want to reach birth mothers and share with them how they can live their lives feeling proud of this painful and unselfish act, rather than ashamed. The first words given to me from my daughter, through a liaison worker, were, "Thank you for loving me so much as to give me a chance at life. It was the most unselfish act anyone has ever done for me and could have only been done with love. I love you and I thank you."

We birth mothers have a hidden self, a self that feels shamed and condemned. It was the first time in twenty-six years that someone understood that it was love, not rejection, that enabled me to relinquish my baby.

As the initial intensity of a reunion begins to wear thin, some birth parents and adoptees decide to take a step back to regain some objectivity. Rishy Powell says she and her son Steve followed this route after the strains between them became unbearable:

We had an estrangement of nine months. When reality set in, and we started to see the warts, I started to see things I didn't like and got scared. I wanted him to be like my other children, but it just didn't happen. I felt that way because I carried him for nine months and there was more of a bond for me than for him. I have other children to compare him to; he didn't have anyone to compare me to. When I gave him up it was a tearing away for me, but it was a different kind of separation for him. Steve also saw things he didn't like, and we both said a few things. He told his wife and she phoned me. She said a few things that weren't right. I wrote her a letter and she never responded.

I think we needed the nine-month separation. We had to step back and take a look at what was going to be long-term. Did we want this? How were we going to handle it? What kind of relationship did we want? In those nine months that's what I was able to determine.

Knowing what I know now, I realize you have to be prepared for a reunion. It does take time, and it should.

Once we came back together it was a more relaxed and comfortable relationship. It's like a second reunion, but we were prepared. We knew what we wanted, we knew where we were going. Many reunions follow this pattern, and it happens for a reason — so you can step back and take a look.

At that time, when we were reunited for the second time, my youngest son was going with a woman he was going to marry, and he told me she was pregnant with twins. He said he was going to marry her, but after she had the babies. I felt threatened because this woman was pregnant with my grandchildren and I was worried that when she had them they would be taken away because my son wasn't married to her. She was able to walk around pregnant, not married, and I resented that because I hadn't been able to; I had had to hide. When the babies were born I couldn't bond with them for two or three months. I was afraid that, because they weren't married, the babies would be taken away from me at any time. I couldn't handle that; I didn't want to handle that. That's when I had my breakdown.

Afterwards I was able to bond with my grandchildren, and everything started coming together for me. I was able to look into myself and accept myself for what I am.

I now have a support group for adoptees and birth parents, and we're well into our second year.

Deborah Andrus's reunion with her birth mother in Winnipeg had been a tearful one, and even though this woman was a stranger, she felt an emotional bond with her. After the initial euphoria, however, Denise began to realize they had different expectations about their future relationship:

My natural mother was very excited about the reunion, and the first afternoon was very informative and comfortable. However, the comfortable feeling dissolved the next day when she phoned all her friends to invite them to come and meet her long-lost daughter. She referred to herself as my mother, and my adoptive mother was expected to be called Faye. She was very aggressive in expressing her desire for me to call her "Mom," and she acted as if she knew everything there was to know about me and not as if we'd just met.

All this behaviour made me very uncomfortable because of my strong bond with my adoptive mother, which had taken twenty-one years to establish. I felt very threatened by her words and actions.

Rebecca Young grew up knowing about her birth family by corresponding with an aunt, and even had faint memories of her birth father visiting her as a young child:

Until I was twenty years old I was content to learn about my birth family from my aunt, but when I met the man I would eventually marry and started to think about having my own family, I found that I had a need to meet them face-to-face.

At this time I wrote to my birth parents and asked if I could meet them. My birth mother was in England visiting relatives so she wasn't there, but I met my two brothers and my father. I have never been so nervous in my whole life! It turned out to be a very pleasant visit but a bit awkward. These people were my own flesh and blood, and they were strangers to me! There was a strong family resemblance physically, but we were different people. My brothers had grown up in extreme poverty and had, at times, been abused, whereas although we weren't rich we always had food to eat, clean clothes to wear and, more importantly, always knew we were loved.

My birth father always wanted to have a relationship with me, and after our meeting talked about me endlessly to the rest of the family, even though we seldom had much communication. In fact, some years later my eldest sister said that she was sick of hearing about me from my father. At first I was hurt by that comment, but then realized she had a legitimate reason to be annoyed. She and my other siblings were the ones who looked after and visited my father once he needed long-term care.

I was a stranger who came and went.

I do have some feelings for my birth family, but it is the brothers and sister I grew up with who are my real family. I think this attitude is one that my birth siblings are comfortable with, but I feel it's troubling to my birth father. I really feel no emotional connection to my birth mother, and I don't think that this causes her too much pain. I think that when I was adopted it was easier for her to ignore my existence. Some people might find that attitude harsh on both her part and mine, but we have come to terms with it, and that is what is important.

In November 1988 my adoptive father died. Since that time I

haven't seen my birth father. I feel that since I can't be the daughter that he wants me to be, then it's easier for everyone if I'm nothing to him.

My children have always known about my "other family" and used to find it odd that other people didn't have three sets of grandparents. Sometimes they tell me I am being cruel not seeing him because they say he is the only father I have left. They don't understand that the only father I ever had died four years ago!

Those who find their birth mother may find themselves comparing her with their adoptive mother. Sharon L. Schwede was always very aware of the differences between her and her adoptive family, both physically and psychologically. She had been struggling with this identity problem for some time, as her adoptive mother supplied the role model of what she considered a woman to be:

I knew how different I was but found myself constantly trying to fit her image. After finding my birth mother — who is bright, funny, outgoing, very loving and beautiful — I felt it was now okay to be who I was. In fact, it was wonderful.

In finding my mother I found myself. It is as if there is an invisible umbilical cord that connects you forever. My mother is like my soulmate, my very dear friend, with whom I can share my deepest feelings. She is not my "mother," the one I grew up with, who cared for me when I was sick, baked for my school functions and cheered me on in my school races. I love my mothers — so very different and so very much a part of who I am.

Paula Matthews felt similarly, that not knowing her birth mother was like having a jigsaw with a piece missing. However, when they did finally meet, Paula experienced a shift in her own response:

The meeting was, at first, a success. My impression now is that she is insecure and unable to dictate her own way of life. I feel she needs me (or someone) to sort her life out, but I don't really feel close enough to her to do it. She has indicated that she would like to move in with me, and I have only met her once. I am not ready for this.

Linda Donovan Evans had occasional contact with her birth mother as she grew up in Moncton, New Brunswick. She says, "Perhaps knowing from an early age who my birth mother was has cleared the murky waters":

When I was seventeen my adoptive parents provided me with a train ticket to visit my birth mother in Toronto. They didn't hesitate to grant my wish, but I could tell they were very apprehensive and concerned and, given my home life, probably afraid that I wouldn't return once I got there. As they set me on the train it was almost as if they were saying goodbye.

I spent two weeks in Toronto. It was fun, and the family was wonderful and kind. Her husband accepted me as one of his own, and the children had been told who I was. My birth mother was as ecstatic as a mother cat who had finally found the errant kitten that had strayed away.

But I hadn't gone to bond and didn't do so. This woman was indeed a stranger. Someday I could be her friend, but not her daughter. She had brought me into the world; she hadn't given me life. I did, however, summon up enough courage to enquire about my birth father and the story of how I had arrived in this world.

My birth father was from Moncton, New Brunswick, and a well-known entertainer with a Country and Western band that had its own television program at the time. I remember my adoptive father forcing me to watch a Country and Western TV show, which I hated.

Knowing who my father was satisfied me. I didn't seek him out. I didn't confront him with my "great news." Like my birth mother, he had brought me into this world, but he didn't raise me.

My birth mother returned to live in Moncton the summer my first son was born. Her first stop was my home, to see her grandson. I was polite and kind, but distant. I could allow her into my life as an acquaintance, but not as a mother. My adoptive mother deserves the job, for she was the one who nurtured me, cared for me through a sickly childhood and put up with my teenage years. I still maintain my distance from my birth mother. I call her on her birthday, and she calls me on mine. I am always welcome to visit but could count on my hand the number of times I have done so.

I have run into my birth father a number of times over the years, but have never introduced myself to him as his daughter. I think he knows exactly who I am, for on the rare occasions I have met him he is cordial and interested. If I were sure he knew who I was, I would introduce myself as his daughter and leave it at that, but I'm not sure. He has his life, and I have mine. We do share musical ability, though, and have even shared the same stage twice recently at variety shows.

For the last five years I have breakfasted at the same restaurant in Moncton every Friday. My birth father has also done so since retiring a couple of years ago. We never exchange hellos. It seems odd, and yet what would we have to share?

If the adoptee has had a difficult life, finding birth relations can be the relief for which they yearned. Although Jaqueline Ackroyd's birth mother had died before she located her birth family, she was overjoyed to meet her cousin and aunt. Her life as an adoptee had been harsh, so she had a special need to feel she belonged:

These were people who loved me, warts and all, as I always imagined a family should. I look so like the photos of my mother, and it emerged more and more that we liked the same things and, in fact, our lives are not so dissimilar. I feel as if I know her, I've been told so much.

I visited my family last weekend, and we exchanged Christmas presents and cards, and hugs and kisses. The pride I felt in telling people I was going to see my aunt and cousin cannot be described.

They phone me every week and insist on calling me Jaqueline, which is the name my mother gave me, not my adoptive name. Strangely enough, I don't feel any regrets about not finding them before. I believe in fate and everything having its allotted time and place. Two months ago was the right time.

I belong, I have a family, they love me, and I am no longer alone.

Having completed a successful search, Gordon Henderson finds that he no longer blames everything on the fact that he was adopted.

I feel that it accounted for all my depressions, my heavy drinking, my experiments with drugs in my younger days. Everything, I felt, must stem back to that because that was day one. Now I realize that it was only one thing in my life. It's like unravelling a ball of yarn. The successful search was the first part of unravelling that ball, or skinning an onion, and there was layer upon layer which had nothing directly to do with adoption. I feel more complete now.

For Lynne Jennex, who found her birth mother and completed a reunion, it had been the right thing to do:

There will always be space in my life for my birth mother. But as for my parents, they are my parents and always will be. They did something special, they took me into their lives and loved me like one of their own and not because they had to, but because they wanted to. Because of that I will never feel like an adopted child.

Since finding her birth mother, Sheila Smith's entire life has altered:

I have become more outgoing, more decisive, more confident, more secure. Even my physical appearance has changed dramatically. It is as if I feel a part of things now. I feel grounded, as if I come from somewhere. I know who I am.

This is not to say that my search and reunion has been without difficulty and pain. On the contrary. But it has been facing that very process that has led to such significant rewards.

For Paul Patterson, too, the reunion with his birth mother Pat was more than he could ever have hoped for:

Getting to know Pat has been a lot better than a lot of people predicted it would be. There's no generation gap at all. There are things I would say to her that I wouldn't say to my mother. A lot of people suggested that if I lived with her it would be a major mistake and we would grow to hate each other. We've had our ups and downs, but tell me what family hasn't. We definitely haven't had as many as I did with my other parents. Now, I think it's stable and it's grown to its peak.

After a lifetime of resentment towards her birth mother, Leona Darling has been able to set that aside and develop a friendship with her. Knowing her birth family has brought a new richness to her life, although all the loose ends will never be completely tied:

An adoptee, growing up not knowing his history, has no real identity. When you learn your history the puzzle pieces are all put into place, and it is very comforting to know where you supposedly belong. However, as an adopted child, you never truly belong in the extended adoptive family, and when you meet your birth family you don't really belong there either. They have a history that you were not a part of, and you can be perceived as an intruder, if you aren't very careful.

All my life I have felt that I've always been on the outside looking in. However, I feel very fortunate that I was raised by such a wonderful family and, now that they have passed on, I have been given the opportunity to develop a relationship with my birth family.

After finding out that she was adopted when she was seven, Jas Wilson feels that the secrecy surrounding it set her off on a self-destructive course, one that was only corrected after a friend put her in touch with NORCAP and she located her birth mother.

My adoptive parents don't know that I have met my "natural mother," nor do I want them to know. It was something I had to do, and I'm a much better person for it, more self-confident; and, more importantly, I get on so much better with my adoptive parents. To me they are my mom and dad.

The reason for telling you part of my story is because I want people to be more open about adoption. It's nothing to be ashamed of for any of the parties involved. It took me twenty years from the day I found those adoption papers finally to understand the whole meaning of adoption and to realize how lucky I was to have two wonderful people to be my parents. If only people had been more open with me when I was seven years old, things might have been different. At least I survived that personal nightmare, thanks to that very special friend.

When Pattie Greening began to suffer from debilitating depression, she decided to discover her roots to see if it was a genetic disorder that ran in her birth family. Her local Adoption Services agency was no help, so she and her husband did the research themselves and were able to find both her birth mother and father. Her story is truly an extraordinary one:

My biological father and I communicate all the time, and I have learned so much, but there is still so much more to learn. I discovered that my biological mother has been treated for depression. Her relationship with her boyfriend had not been a good one for the last few years. She said that her life was much better now that I was in it.

She also told me that she was still very much in love with my biological father. She never fell out of love with him, and she always wished for the day that she would find us. She told me she wanted to see him and would move in with him in a flash, or marry him in a second. She would leave everything she had and go to him.

She got his phone number from me, and after she talked with him she said she was going to see him again. She went, and they both sound so happy. My biological father said he always loved her as well. Everything is going perfectly, and they intend to stay together. According to my mother they are going to marry in the very near future. I guess this was meant to be, but I never thought in a million years that by my locating my biological parents I would bring them together again after twenty-two years apart. It's like a fairy tale come true.

Whether a successful search brings good news or bad, the lives of those involved will never be the same again. When Patricia McCarron had her reunion with her birth mother she learned her mother's pregnancy was the result of being raped by a masked assailant. She also learned that there was a strong history of cancer in her birth family and that her mother was in remission from a second bout of leukemia:

My first reaction to this "information overload" once I got home was one of fear, due to the history of cancer in her family. This blocked out any thoughts I might have been having about the news that my birth father was a rapist. That was one scenario I had never considered.

My counsellor, Judith Kizell, put it all in perspective for me when she told me that rape is not a gene that can be inherited like medical conditions. She surmised the attacker was probably under the influence of alcohol and just out for a "good time." I needed to hear that! Since then I've reconciled myself to accepting the circumstances of my birth, and I've come to the conclusion that it's his loss — he'll never get to know me as a daughter.

When Deborah Andrus was reunited with her birth father, she met a severe alcoholic:

I have chosen to break ties with my birth parents until my children are a little older and able to understand the differences in lifestyles. Despite my findings throughout my search and reunions with my birth parents — not very positive findings — I don't regret this experience. It has only reinforced my feelings of love, trust and respect that I have for my adoptive parents and for the job they did raising my brothers, my sister and myself.

Sheila Smith says that now she and her birth mother are coming out of their initial "honeymoon period," some sensitive issues are coming to the surface:

To have found my birth mother to be an alcoholic, looking after her brother who is also an alcoholic, and to have it insinuated that I am responsible for the ill health of my birth grandmother, and then asked if I was going to take responsibility and move out west to look after them all, was not at all a part of my hopes, my dreams and my fantasy. Yet discovering a genetic link to my own alcoholism has been perhaps the greatest comfort I have ever known, while it also allows for empathy and understanding for the situation as a whole.

After having to adjust to finding her son in prison, Margaret King still had to deal with more unexpected bad news. As their relationship developed, Margaret's deep love for him was sorely tested:

Over the next few weeks we visited him frequently in the halfway house and talked on the phone. We lent him money to pay off some fines from before he was incarcerated. He and I pored over family photo albums. He gave me pictures of my granddaughter. He was allowed no contact with her because of his past. He hoped to gain visiting rights in the future.

He found work at a local shop and attended counselling. On some occasions I attended with him. He had been sexually abused as a child by an older adoptive brother. One day he called and asked if I would come down and we could talk. He was uneasy. It was hard for him to confess, but he did. He was gay. Shocked? Yes. Hate him? No. I told him it was all right. I said I didn't understand it, but he was still my son and I loved him.

Our relationship continued to grow, but he began to change. He began drinking, then it was drugs. He was due to be released from the halfway house soon, and he was scared. He couldn't live alone, yet found it difficult to live with others. He spoke of his curiosity about the afterlife, suggesting we die together to see if it was true.

One day he turned up at my home with a car. I asked where he had got it, and he claimed a man had given it to him in return for oral sex. Then he claimed he was living with an older homosexual, a man who was quite wealthy and a major drug importer-exporter. I fell for it hook, line and sinker. Then he turned up with a friend and wanted to know if they could stay for a few days. They moved in. For a while it was fun.

My son's moods were terrible. He was beginning to cause problems between my husband and me. He lied constantly and burst out in rage when he was confronted with his lies. I spoke to his parole officer, trying to get help. My son flew at me for sticking my nose in his business. Now he would be returned to prison, he claimed. Again I talked to his parole officer, just to be told he was lying to me again. My son told me he had been to an AIDS clinic and things didn't look good, another lie — he had been to a psychiatrist's office. He was doing drugs and drinking, so finally I issued an ultimatum. He had two weeks to get himself sorted out or move.

He slept in his car for a few days, then seemed to snap out of it. He had met a new "friend." He claimed they were wildly involved, but it wasn't true. His good mood lasted a while, then we had a huge fight and he left. Then the letters started — angry, hateful, threatening letters. This went on for two months, then nothing. Finally we were able to talk and agreed to start again. He was going to move to the West Coast and try to find a new life, a fresh start. I agreed it might be for the best.

Then he called me with the news that he had been diagnosed HIV positive. He was crying; he wanted to come home. I was floored; he sounded so sincere. I found him a room and paid for it for two weeks until he could get social assistance. He settled into his new room and soon found a new "companion." Then the hotel he was living in was closed. They had nowhere to go so they moved in with us again. Again, things went well for a while. Then he slipped back into his nasty side and was bent on creating problems. I discovered he was giving my youngest boy drugs.

He and his friend found their own place. We helped them move and gave them household necessities. A week later I was told I was welcome to visit but not my husband. He stated that he hated him, that he was an asshole and was using me. I never went back.

Once again the calls started. My youngest son began to withdraw, then moved in with his brother. At Christmas my birth son sent a note in a card, suggesting we try to make amends. I wrote back and told him I was willing to talk, on neutral ground. He never replied. My youngest son returned home, saying that his brother's friend had made sexual advances towards him.

We had no contact from that point on. He told his adoptive parents that my husband and I were harassing him. He called the police and claimed my husband had a coat like the one found near a woman's burnt body, and another time told them we tried to run him over. I have had detectives on my doorstep checking out my son's alibi regarding a double homicide he was implicated in. I have had an investigator from the police sitting at my table because of a phone call my son made to me telling me of a girl's stabbing death eight hours before her body was found.

Sounds unbelievable? I wish it was untrue. These same officers have told me they believed my family and I may be in danger. We have had security lights put on the property and alarms on the doors. At one point during a wild car ride, my son threatened to drown me. When I laughed he said I wouldn't be laughing when he bound my hands and tied blocks to my feet.

I've since learned that my son was diagnosed as a socio-path/psychopath several years earlier. I've read everything I can find on this. I needed to know what caused it. Opinions vary — some say genetics, some say early childhood trauma. But one thing is unanimous — these people have no conscience, no remorse, and feel nothing for anyone but themselves. Now I can believe him when he stated that if I were killed it wouldn't bother him. As for the girl who was stabbed to death, they couldn't connect him to it. The double homicide has never been solved. I don't know, part of me says yes — he was in that city that day;

part of me says no — my child couldn't be that cruel, that cold-hearted.

Am I sorry I found him? No. I'll always be glad that I was able to find him. It gave me peace to know he had been raised by good people who did all they were able to do for him. Do I advise others to search? I can't say Don't. I believe my son and I are the exception. But I do advise people to go slowly, don't just dive in as I did and believe all you are told. Remember, this child may be yours biologically, but he wasn't raised with your principles and values, and even if his adoptive parents share your values there's no guarantee the child does. And find out as much as possible before meeting. I believe social agencies should divulge what they learn of the child if possible.

I'm sorry for the anguish my family has endured because of this young man's behaviour. For a while our home was very unstable. My son is a manipulative, cunning, selfish, uncaring person . . . but we are recovering.

Ann Ashley was adopted herself and had hoped her daughter Sherry had been raised in a home as good as her adoptive mother had provided for her. After meeting Sherry, however, Ann heard the news that birth mothers dread:

I'd like to say that Sherry had a good life with loving adoptive parents, but it wasn't true. She feels she was adopted to keep her mother company while her father was sent to Cyprus by the armed forces. She was physically and mentally abused and wonders why someone at school didn't step in when she continually attended with black eyes and noticeable bruises.

Her adoptive parents never told anyone Sherry was adopted. Her adoptive mother went so far as to complain to everyone how hard her pregnancy was and that she almost died in labour. Sherry's uncle told her at eighteen that he thought she was adopted. She asked her parents, and they threw her adoption papers at her and told her I'd never want to see her anyway.

If I'd only known, I would have tried to get her back somehow. I know this is probably an isolated case, but I do feel there should be longer follow-up by social workers.

Patty Stover has been reunited with her birth daughter and, although they still feel like strangers, they're hoping to develop a relationship:

No matter what the outcome of the relationship, I am glad I had this reunion. I feel as if I have been let out of a dark cupboard. For the first time in my life, I don't care what people think of me — I finally know that I was not such a bad person. A lot of unanswered questions have finally been solved; my dreams for my birth daughter have turned into reality, thanks to the family with whom she was placed.

My birth daughter is from a middle-class family who provided her with all kinds of opportunities to grow and develop into the beautiful, mature young lady she is today. I do feel that I am very lucky that she had that chance. It doesn't always turn out the way we picture it. If her family environment had been unstable and unloving, I am sure our reunion would not have been as happy.

I have finally opened up and told a few friends; some are in a similar situation. The few I have talked to said they were too afraid to search. Since hearing about my reunion they now feel they can take that first step out of the cupboard. We had almost no options back then, so it is time we stop blaming ourselves.

Roxanne Cochrane did not have a conventional reunion, as she had kept in contact with her birth daughter throughout the child's formative years. Roxanne had had no intention of giving up her daughter at birth, but she was hospitalized with complications, and a childless couple who were taking care of the infant begged to keep her:

In 1990 her parents called. A lot had been going on that I knew nothing about. Karla wasn't going to school but was running away and had spent time in a psychiatric ward on two separate occasions. She'd also shoplifted, made sure she got caught, and told the judge she thought if she were bad enough they'd send her to me!

She spent two weeks here that November and ten weeks this past summer. I took her to meet all my family, as well as her father and his family. She asked question upon question. Her adoptive parents had done everything for her all her life — I had to teach her how to fry an egg, to wash clothes, and this child was sixteen years old. She said she hated her adoptive parents, and we tried to work through that.

She's been back with them for seven months. I get a letter once a month or so. We call on special occasions. I have to assume things are okay. They say they are. She says she tolerates them but loves me and understands why she was adopted.

It's not always a happy story. My life's been great. I got better physically. I had six weeks to change my mind after I signed her adoption paper, but it was done and I accepted that and went on with my life. Since my marriage I've discovered I can't have more children — it happens often after giving your first up for adoption. It was no big deal.

Karla, on the other hand, is having a problem with being adopted. She still has a lot of questions and is seeing counsellors for a major problem with self-esteem. Her parents are now close to sixty. They're scared — they've admitted they feel too old to deal with a teenager. At one point they offered to pay me to take her. They sometimes look to me for guidance, and I don't need that. She's too far away for me to enforce a curfew.

Although at first Maureen Dinner's birth mother could not face the trauma of seeing her daughter, Maureen persisted and was able to get to know her. It has been a positive experience, but there are still some unresolved feelings:

Our relationship is a good one. I think we are good friends. We see each other a fair bit and talk on the phone more, as distance is sometimes a factor.

My mother can never forgive herself for what she did. She can't believe she could have ever given up her daughter. She has so much regret and thinks a lot of what might have been. She never had other children because she thought that if she couldn't bring me up then it would be unfair to bring other children into this world.

My birth mother's family have never known she was even pregnant. My maternal grandmother is eighty years old, and my birth mother isn't going to tell her of my existence. In fact, she isn't going to tell any of her family about me. Apart from telling one friend, I am the secret she still carries with her.

To be honest, this part bothers me the most. Part of me wanted to be met with open arms and introduced to her family and welcomed into it, but I know that will never happen. When I think how far we've come, I guess I should settle for that.

To Karen Kloosterman's joy, she has met her birth mother and the huge extended family on her birth father's side of the family. She reflects on what finding them has meant to her life:

I met countless relatives! It was exhausting physically, mentally and emotionally, but definitely worth it. I felt very comfortable with them, almost as if I'd known them all my life. They welcomed me as one of the family and accepted me for who I am.

My puzzle is becoming more and more complete as the pieces

are slowly being put together, and I feel more at peace with myself. On the other hand, it's a very emotional experience, a real rollercoaster. There are highs, but there are lows as well. My birth family seems to be almost constantly on my mind, and while I would like to spend a lot of time with them, I find I need to be by myself as well, just to sort out all my thoughts.

Finding one's birth parents is not the solution to all one's problems, but rather helps the individual to identify them, put them in their proper perspective, understand how to cope with them and see whether the problem is related to their adoption or not. It's easy to blame things on one's adoption, to heap all one's anger, hurt and need to be loved on that one fact. It's a growing experience to learn how to cope with these feelings and to separate them from just everyday living.

I look forward to what the future will bring me regarding my birth family. It's not always easy, but it is definitely worth it. My birth mother told me in our first conversation of how she talked to me during the brief ten days in the hospital, when I was born. She said, "I would look into your big dark eyes and tell you not to ever, ever forget me. And you would look up at me so trustingly. . . ." Maybe this explains my deep desire to know my mother. I know I'd do it again.

For Pat Tyler, who relinquished her son Paul, the conclusion is a happy one. But to reach it they both had to recognize the fact that each had suffered:

Paul resented me expressing my pain, as do a lot of adoptees. They really don't accept that the pain the birth mother experiences may be in excess of theirs.

Paul lives with us now, and I have since adopted him. You can adopt an adult. He is no longer legally the child of his adoptive parents; he is legally my child. We didn't tell his adoptive parents that.

The hardest thing for me was meeting his adoptive parents. I quite liked them, and they were very nice to me, and I appreciated that. I love them because they are the parents who raised him. But I also hate them, if you can understand that, because they had what was really mine. What gave them the right to have my child? Because I was poor? They recognized that meeting me was a good emotional experience for Paul.

Paul wanted me to adopt him. It's not that I didn't want to do it; this was great. In my opinion adopting him was setting the record straight and giving him back what he was entitled to.

I never fantasized about my son. The only fantasy was being together again with his father, me and him. I always felt like part of a fragmented family — Paul's father was somewhere, who knew where; Paul was somewhere; who knew where, but nevertheless there was this relationship, a very intangible triangle between the three of us that will always be there. I always thought that, in a way, we were a family, even though legally and emotionally that wasn't the case.

Pat's son Paul Patterson echoes the same feelings. The realization that each had suffered in their own way was important:

I think it was a comparison of pain. There was a lot of competition: whose pain was worse? You only know your own pain, so each one thinks their pain is worse. I think there are more genetic biological connections with your birth parents than anyone has any idea about. I've seen it for myself. We've both laughed at things and said, "I knew you were going to do that," or, "I knew you were going to say that." Why? Because I would have done the same thing.

I've met quite a few cousins, aunts, uncles and friends, and it was a lot to deal with at first. I realize Pat wants to show me off, which is understandable. It was strange meeting my relatives because they wouldn't really talk to me; they interrogated me. I don't mind a conversation, but I had problems with that. I guess they felt that they could do it because they are now related to me.

I mentioned that to Pat, so at the next family gathering no one said anything to me! I took Pat aside afterwards and said, "At first it was too much, but now everyone's afraid to talk to me. This is crazy!" Since then it seems a little better.

The first night I met Pat I showed her photographs of me growing up. It was really hard for her. At first she didn't want to see them because they were pictures she should have taken. In one way she loves my adoptive parents, but at the same time she hates them. They did the raising of me which she didn't. I gave her my family album, and every night she'd look at all those pictures. I had to take it away from her because she was obsessed with looking at them.

Now when we sit up late it's almost getting boring. It was so intense before because it was a new experience. It's been very interesting, and I'm very, very glad I found her.

I have since gone back to my original name and have been adopted by Pat. So I've been adopted twice. I haven't told my adoptive parents. I feel that maybe someday I will, but right now I haven't come to that decision. When Pat adopted me, we went into the judge's chambers, and he looked at the papers and said, "In all my years of being on the bench, I've never seen anything quite like this. I'd be honoured to sign it." It's hard because all my friends call me by my original name. I'm still trying to make the transition, which isn't easy. All of a sudden I have a different first and last name.

My last birthday was the first birthday I spent with Pat. It was really good because all my other birthdays were no big deal to me because of being adopted. I'd always sneak off, and I didn't want people around me. It wasn't a full celebration. It would remind me I was adopted and make me wonder where my birth mother was. It was something I didn't really want to think about.

The first birthday Rishy Powell shared with her son she gave him a special gift to peel back the years:

I gave him a rattle and a duck, along with a regular present. For every year that I missed I also gave him a gift. It was my way of making up.

Rishy Powell had been forced to hide in her family's apartment during her pregnancy and even managed to keep the secret from her father. Now that Steve was back in her life, it was time to tell her father the news:

When I was reunited with Steve, he, his wife and two kids were here for Passover. I told my other son, if his grandfather asked who these people were, to say that Steve was his friend whose parents were away for the holidays so they had come here. So, for the first night of Passover I sat Steve and his wife on the same side as my father, with the kids sort of at an angle. My father asked my son who they were, and he answered as we'd agreed.

The next night I sat them across from my father so now he had to look at them. After they left the second night, I said to my father, "You know Larry's friends? Do you think the man looked like me?" He said, "Yes, he did look a little like you, and the girl did, too. Who are they?"

I said, "Daddy, I have something to tell you." This is thirty-four years later. "I had a child before I was married." He kept saying, "I didn't know, I didn't know." That was all he said, and he accepted it. He was eighty-two.

Steve Tobis showed great compassion towards his birth mother Rishy, but there were still problems to be faced:

I never felt rejected by Mom because I'd always thought she was dead. I found out why she gave me up. The hard part for Mom to deal with was the fact that I understood. It made complete, logical sense to me. Mom had a hard time coping with the fact that I understood! She couldn't handle the guilt of having given me up. I told her, "I understand and it's okay. You gave me up for all the right reasons. You had no choice."

Prior to this Mom had asked where this relationship was going, and I said, "You know, Mom, I don't want another mother. I already have a mother, but I want you to be my friend."

Once you're reunited there should be a support group you go to together to get over some of the problems you may have. That way you could both air your feelings. When I went to meetings before the reunion, it really didn't matter what the woman said to me. She said that a lot of times reunions work out; a lot of times they don't. Don't have your expectations too high, etc. But when the time comes, you don't even think of it. You go in head first, and it's all exciting and it's all a bed of roses, and unless you have the support there after you're reunited, for both people, that bed of roses can easily turn into a tumbleweed.

Ann Ashley tried living with her birth parents after their reunion — it was either that or going back to reform school:

I knew from day one that it wouldn't work, but I stayed for three months because I really liked the school I was in. My birth father had a good job, but he was a very loud, obnoxious man who drank a lot. He was abusive to my birth mother, who is very quiet and passive. I told my social worker, but she didn't listen, so one day I just hitchhiked to my adoptive mother's sixty miles away. I was given the choice to go back or go to reform school. I chose the latter. I had some contact with my birth mother and father, but it was very limited.

My birth father died five years ago of lung cancer. I sent him a card when he was sick, but I didn't go to see him or go to the funeral. I sometimes regret it now. It wasn't that he didn't treat me well; I just didn't trust him somehow.

Liz Vineberg White found her daughter in 1985 after registering with ALMA:

She was a dysfunctional person, which I find so many birth mothers and adoptees are, because they don't fit. Adoptees are led to feel abandoned on purpose, as if there was some kind of choice in the matter. It was a good reunion in that we exchanged information. I know she had a good upbringing, very good parents, every emotional and economic opportunity was there for her — she just chose not to take it. We don't have any contact now, and that's all right because she knows where I live and can contact me when she's comfortable with it. She may have the "good adoptee" syndrome, I don't know, where they feel very disrespectful or as if they are cheating their adoptive parents by searching or accepting the object of their search. I just sit and wait; I'm not pushing.

Joan Marshall set off to find her birth family and found what most adoptees are hoping to discover when they decide to search:

I found me. I had a chance to resolve a lot of things — the curiosity, the medical issues, the identity issues.

My birth mother is eighty-seven and is a very independent person. A lot of my survival skills come from her, and it's just marvellous because I was adopted into a family that gave me a very traditional upbringing in terms of a woman's role. I'm not like that, and my birth mother isn't like that either. It's great to see that in my birth mother, and it has alleviated my feeling guilty for not being the "good wife."

Gordon Henderson is married with a family of his own. After having found his birth mother, he is a changed person:

I feel far more complete. Previously, whenever I was with other people and someone looked at me, I wondered if they knew who I was, because I didn't. Now I know who I am.

And as her relationship with her birth mother Josie has developed, Jan Rourke realizes she made the right decision in finding her:

In a way I have two families now. No one will ever replace Mom; she is, always has been and always will be, my mother. Yet no one else could ever take that special part of my heart that belongs to Josie. I know that in a strictly physical sense I would not exist without her, but she plays a much more important role in my life than that. In more ways than even she realizes, she helped to make me what I am.

I feel very fortunate to have two such special mothers in my life. I wish every adoptee who seeks out a birth parent could be so lucky.

Appendix

The following is a list — by no means exhaustive — of groups and organizations that may be able to assist you in a search for your birth family and provide emotional and practical support.

Canada
Parent Finders, Metropolitan Toronto Area
2279 Yonge Street, Suite 11, Toronto, Ontario M4P 2C7
(416) 486-8346

Parent Finders Edmonton
#49-52307 Range Road 213, Sherwood Park, Alberta T8G 1C1
(403) 922-5023

Searchline
63 Holborn Avenue, Nepean, Ontario K2C 3H1
(613) 825-1640

Parent Finders, National Capital Region
P.O. Box 5211, Station F, Ottawa, Ontario K2C 3H5
(613) 238-8305

Adoption Disclosure Register, Ministry of
Community & Social Services
2 Bloor Street, 24th Floor, Toronto, Ontario M4W 3H8
(416) 327-4730

Great Britain
National Organization for the Counselling
of Adoptees and Parents
(NORCAP), 3 New High Street, Headington, Oxford OX3 7AJ
0865-750554

General Register Office,
St. Catherine's House, 10 Kingsway, London WC2B 6JP

The Registrar General, Adopted Children's Register
Titchfield, Fareham, Hants PO15 5RR
or
New Register House, Edinburgh EH1 3YT
or
Oxford House, 49-55 Chichester Street, Belfast BT1 4HL

Post-Adoption Centre
8 Torriano Mews, Torriano Avenue, London NW5 2RZ
071-284-0555

Natural Parents' Support Group (NPSG)
3 Aldergrove, Normanton, West Yorkshire WF6 1LF
0924-894-076

Parent to Parent Information Adoption Services (PPIAS)
Lower Boddington, Daventry, Northamptonshire NN11 6YB
0327-60295

United States
Council for Equal Rights in Adoption
401 East 74th Street, Suite 17D, New York, NY 10021
(212) 988-0110

American Adoption Congress
Suite 9, 1000 Connecticut Avenue, N.W., Washington, DC 20036
1 (800) 274-6736

The Musser Foundation
P.O. Box 1860, Cape Coral, FL 33910
(813) 542-1342
1 (800) 477-SEEK

Healing Adoptees
66 Stockade Path, Plymouth, MA 02360
(508) 224-3953

ALMA Reunion Registry
P.O. Box 154, Washington Bridge Station, New York, NY 10033
(212) 581-1568

National Adoption Center
1218 Chestnut Street, Philadelphia, PA 19107
(215) 925-0200

First State Search Consultants
P.O. Box 748, Bear, DE 19701-0748
(302) 836-9887

Adoptive Parents for Open Records
P.O. Box 193, Long Valley, NJ 07853

Index

2